Great For Sign Language Interpreters

American Sign Language

Thesaurus

By Don Cabbage, Ph. D.

DON CABBAGE
— PUBLISHING —

ISBN: 978-1-966954-93-4 (paperback)
ISBN: 978-1-966954-94-1 (hardcover)
ISBN: 978-1-966954-95-8 (epub)

Library of Congress Control Number: 2025924726

In ASL there are no Homonyms as are found in oral languages. ASL words have no sound therefore words meaning different things are not alike.

The use of a sign with a particular facial expression can charge inflection of meaning for a word. Change of facial expression can change simple open hands extended in front of the body from a simple "What" to "What????", "What!!!!!!!!!!!!!!", or "What's up".

This text demonstrates that a basic ASL vocabulary of 1,000 words represents several thousand words used in English. One sign in ASL represents most form of any one word in English. For Example: "Run" is a verb and "Running" is a noun. Both words use the same sign in ASL. Represented by one sign are all forms of the word "Weak" . "Weak", "Weakly", "Weakened" are different forms of the same word in English but are represented by one sign in ASL. This principle holds true for the use of root words with suffixes. Prefixes are often a different sign of their own such as "Un-" being represented by the ASL sign "Not" , and "Pre-" represented by the ASL sign "Before".

The 1,000 word vocabulary of ASL I represents many synonyms. For example the ASL sign "Which" can represent several English words such as "Which", "Whether", "Whichever", "Choice", "Doesn't matter" , or "Indifferent-nce".

The learning of American Sign Language expands the student's ability for self expression. It takes language from the oral and aural mediums most common to most of us to a totally different dimension. Constructive manual or physical expression adds immeasurably to the adventure of self-expression. Enjoy the adventure.

Introduction

American Sign Language Thesaurus

Is a companion and expansion of <u>American Sign Language I</u>. It is a study of English Synonyms commonly associated with basic signs of the American Sign Language (ASL). When studying ASL it is important to remember that the language is not a manual form of another language but a distinctive language of its own. ASL has characteristics and distinctive of a linguistic system. Signs express concepts in a manual linguistic form.

Compared to English, ASL express itself general in the most simple and common form of words. ASL words express concepts by manual gesture not by sound. (Be careful. It is easy to hear a spoken term in English and express it in the wrong form of ASL.)

The expression of most ASL words is in the present tense. To speak in various tenses the speaker states the tense of his conversation then speaks in the present tense.

Signs are usually expressed in singular forms. Establish plurality by stating plurality. Using the signs "Many" , "Few" , or "All" may do that. Specific numbers may establish plurality such as in "Two boy".

ASL
Thesaurus

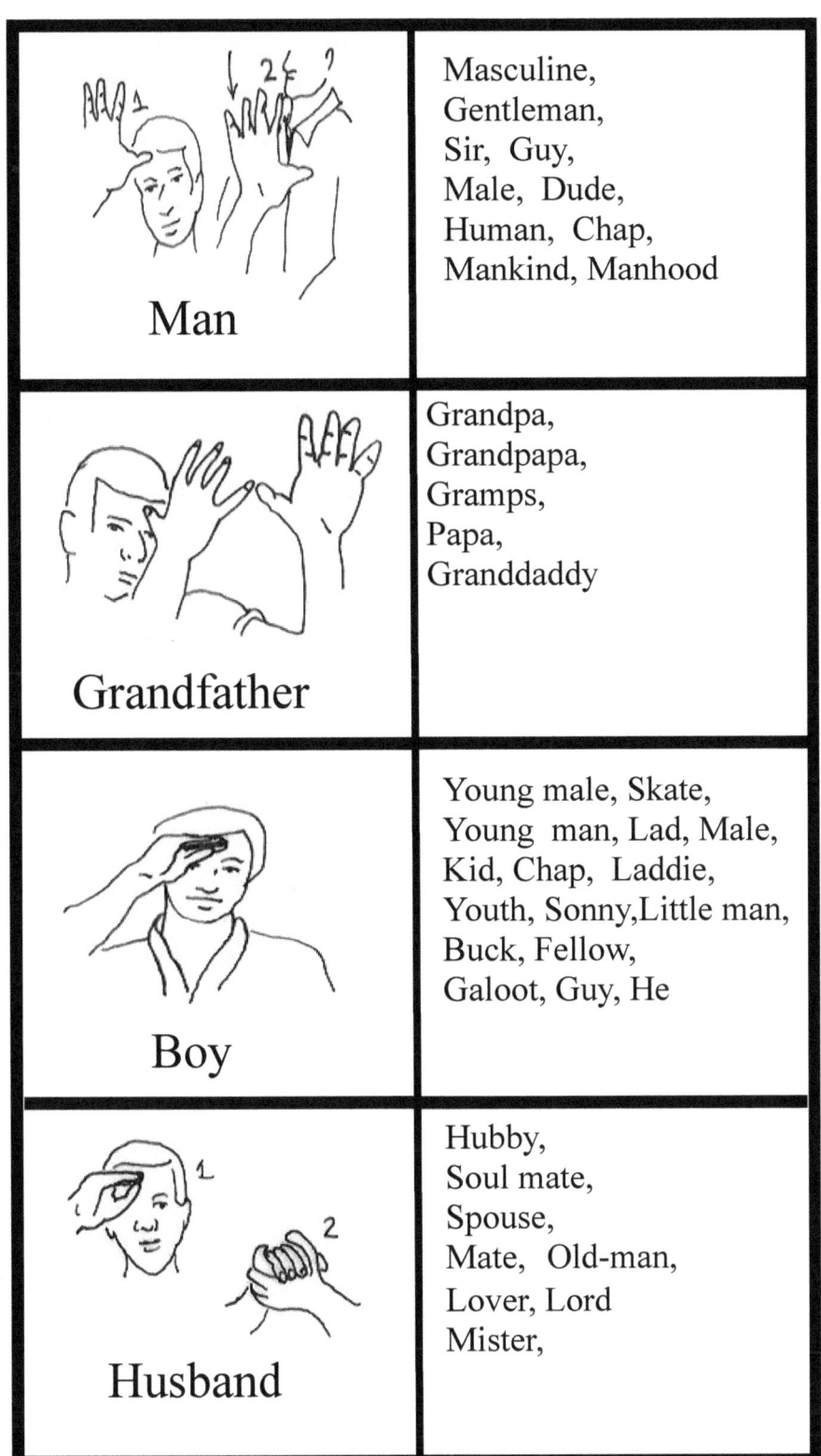

Man	Masculine, Gentleman, Sir, Guy, Male, Dude, Human, Chap, Mankind, Manhood
Grandfather	Grandpa, Grandpapa, Gramps, Papa, Granddaddy
Boy	Young male, Skate, Young man, Lad, Male, Kid, Chap, Laddie, Youth, Sonny, Little man, Buck, Fellow, Galoot, Guy, He
Husband	Hubby, Soul mate, Spouse, Mate, Old-man, Lover, Lord Mister,

Woman	Female, Madame, Mistress, Miss, Lady, Missis, Feminine, Gentlewoman Madam, Chick, Lass,
Mother	Mom, Mommy, Mamma, Ma, Mama Matriarch, Maternal,
Grandmothe r	Old Lady Nana, Grandma, Grams, Granny, Nanny, Ma-Maw, Me-maw
Girl	Lass, Maid. Damsel, Maiden, Female, Daughter, Young woman, Gal, Lassie, Miss, Missy

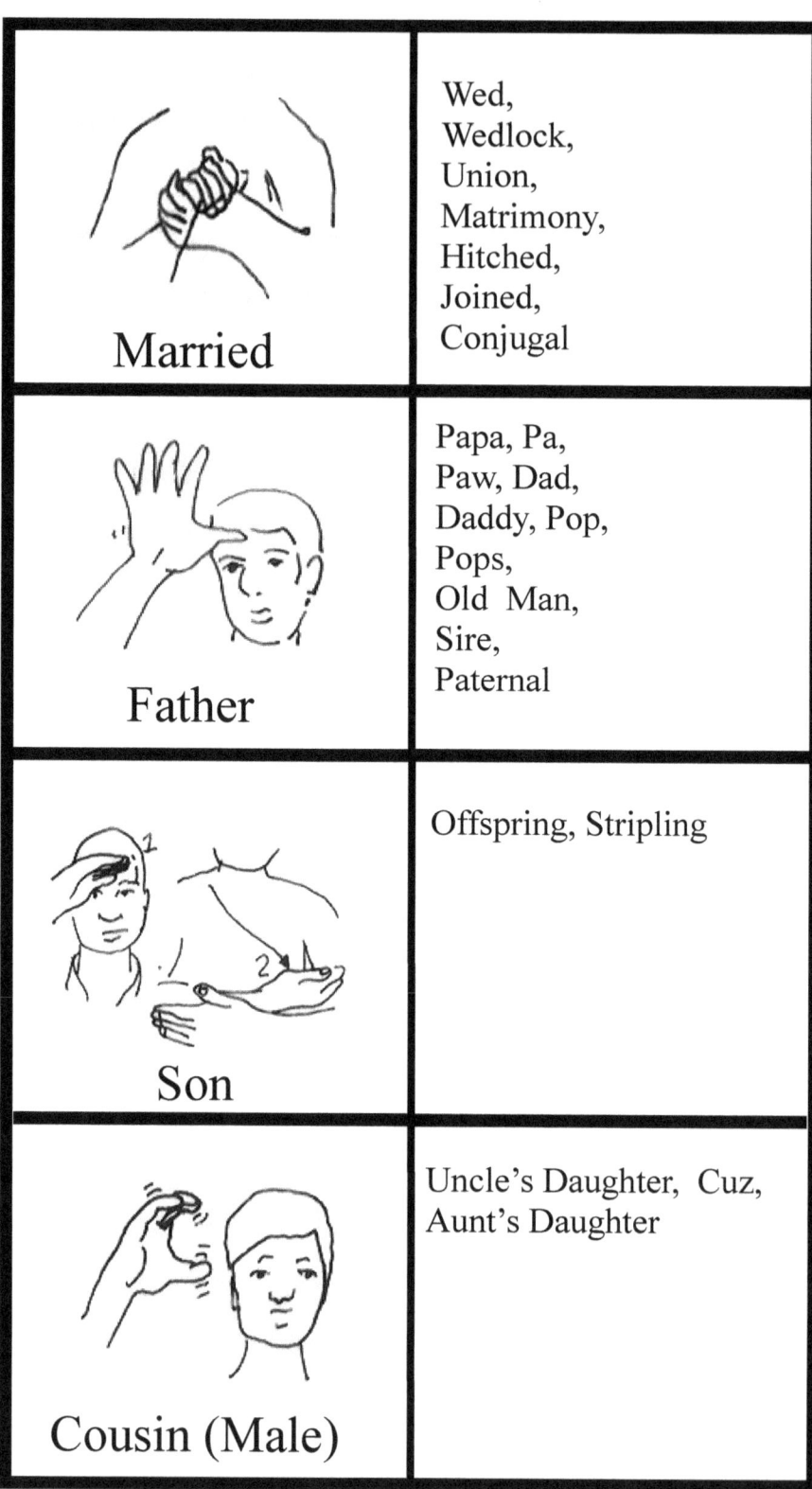

Married	Wed, Wedlock, Union, Matrimony, Hitched, Joined, Conjugal
Father	Papa, Pa, Paw, Dad, Daddy, Pop, Pops, Old Man, Sire, Paternal
Son	Offspring, Stripling
Cousin (Male)	Uncle's Daughter, Cuz, Aunt's Daughter

Father in Law	Dad in law
Son in Law	Daughter's husband
Brother	Sibling, Bro
Sister	Sibling, Sis

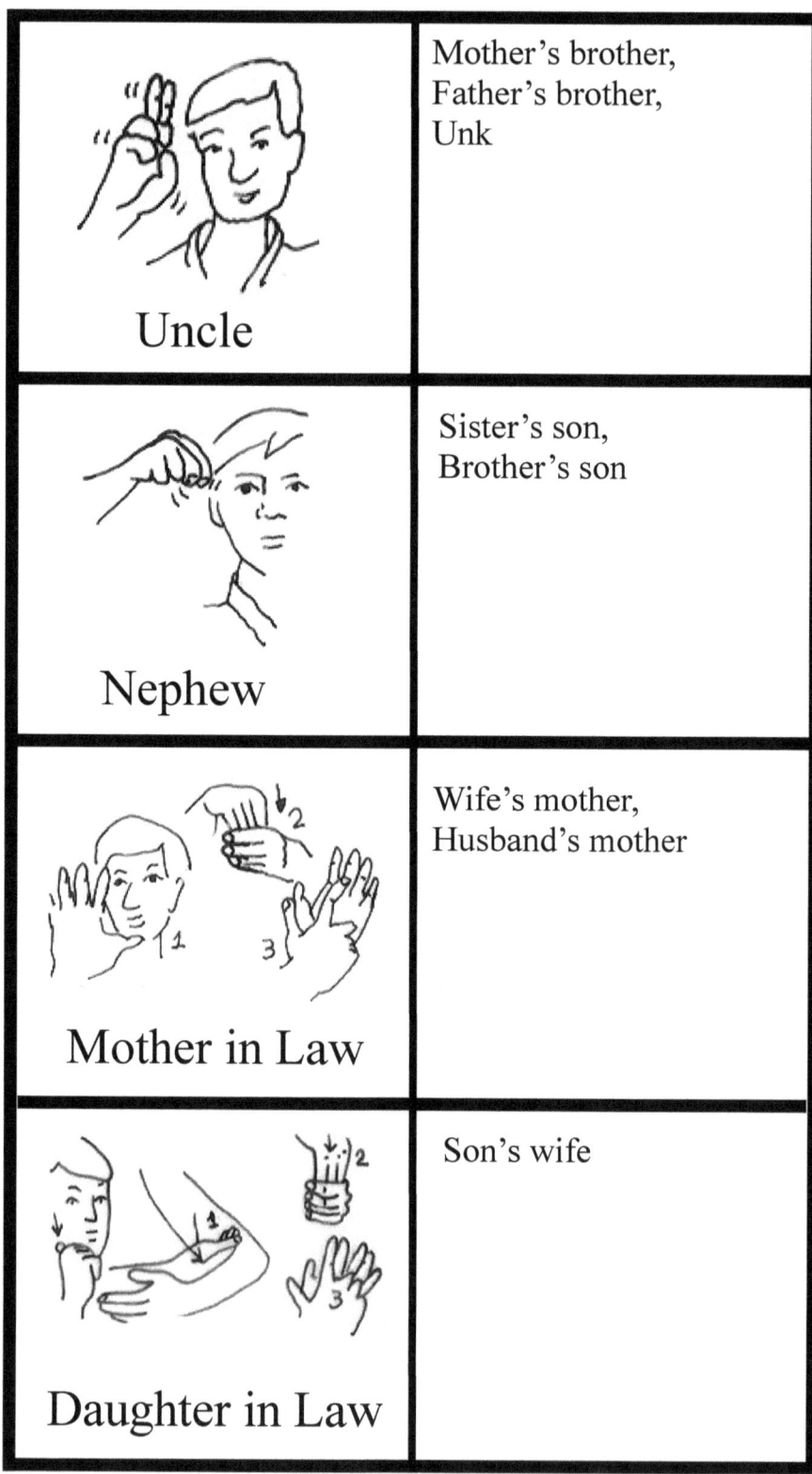

Uncle	Mother's brother, Father's brother, Unk
Nephew	Sister's son, Brother's son
Mother in Law	Wife's mother, Husband's mother
Daughter in Law	Son's wife

Lie	Untruth, Betray, Lied, Fib, Fibber, Deceive, Deceiver, Not truthful, Palter, Prevaricate, Equivocate
True	Sure, Genuine, Valid, Sincere, Really, Absolutely, Positive, Fact, Frankly, Indeed, Certain, Honest, Faithful, Actual, Actually, Certainly, Loyal, Ardent, Fast, Liege, Resolute, Staunch, Steady, Steadfast, To be verb
False	Sham, Pseudo, Fakes, Pretense, Incorrect, Fable, Fiction, Artificial, False Hood, Un-viable, Not true, Malarkey, Untrue, Wrong, Fabricate, Falsely, Faithless, Disloyal, Perfidious, Recreant, Traitorous, Treacherous
Better	Improve, Better than, Greater than, Superior Ameliorate, Amend, Help, Meliorate, Upgrade

Daughter	Lass, Maid, Damsel, Maiden, Female, Daughter, Young woman, Gal, Lassie, Miss, Missy
Wife	Better half, Partner, Soul mate, Spouse, Woman, Mate, Mrs., Old lady, Connubial, Martial, Caught, Mate, Nuptial, Spousal, Wedded, Espousal
Aunt	Auntie, Mother's sister, Father's sister
Cousin (Female)	Cuz, Uncle's daughter, Aunt's daughter

 Once-in-a-while	Now and then, Sometime, Occasionally, On Occasion, From time To time, Not often, Sporadically, Rarely
 Motor, Machine	Engine, Gears, Mechanism, Industry, Manufacture, Machinery, Motor Running, Wheel, Automation, Mill, Plant, Manufacturer
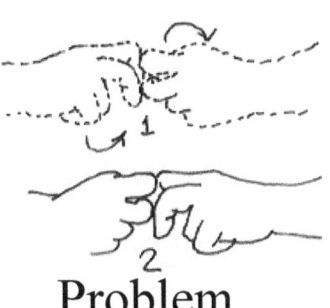 Problem	Difficulty, Trouble, Enigma Difficult Situation, Dilemma, Friction, Puzzled, Riddle, Issue, Perplex, Perplexing, Hard time
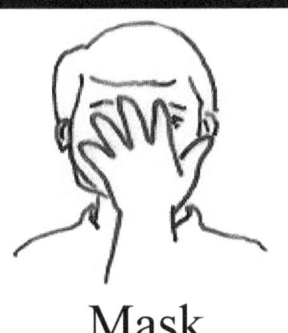 Mask	Cover, Disguise, Embarrassed, Veil, Covering, Pretence, Screen, Masquerade, Halloween, Hide Camouflage, Cloak Dissemble, Dress up, Dissimulation

Paint	Brush, Painting, Painted, Fix up, Whitewash, Cover, Maquillage
Future	Later on, Someday, Eventually, Hereafter, Time to come, By and By, Ahead, Aftertime, Afterward, Offing, To-be
Later	Not now, Later on, After while, Afterward, Not yet, Subsequently, In the future, Eventually, By and By
Law	Authority, Code, Legal, Provision, Scribe, Statue, Mandate, Legislate, Ordinance, Prohibition, Commandment, Structure, Rules, Assize, Principle, Canon, Decree, Discretion, Edict, Precept, Prescript

Quit	Top, Cease, Desist, Discontinue, Halt, Knock it off, Surcease
Vote	Elect, Election, Ballot, Suffrage
Gas	Gasoline, Fuel, Petrol
Against	Prejudice, Oppose, Versus

Commandment	Mandate, Law, Constitute, Rule, Regulation, Commands, Standards
Rule	Guidelines, Regulate, Directions, Standards, Requires, Code, Governs, Maxims, Dominates
Impress	Stress, Spire, Imprint, Show Emphasis, Inspire, Mark, Impression, -ed, -es, Affect, Influence, Move, Sway
Require	Demand, Request, Must Have, Essential, Necessitate

Think	Thought, Consider, Ponder, Reflect, Think about, Reckon, Mediation, Speculate, Wonder, Conceive, Fancy, Suppose, Surmise
Dream	Fancy, Fantasy, Vision, Daydream, Spaced out, Image, Wistful, Out in Space, Subconscious
Crazy	Insane, Mentally impaired, Loony, Loopy, Wacko, Wacky, Nuts, Nutty, Warped, Twisted, Touched, Unsound, psycho, Kooky, Witless, Disordered, Deranged, Foolish, Absurd, Harebrained, Idle headed, Lunatic, Mad, Silly, Crazed, Cuckoo, Screwy, Maniac,
For	What for?, What do you need it for ?

Doubt	Unsure, Question, Unbelief, Skeptical, Uncertain, Not Believe, Misgiving, Disbelief, Confusion, Distrust, Misdoubt, Mistrust, Suspect, Cynical
Goal	Ideal, Objective, Target, Focus, Purpose, Aim, Mission, Finish line, Ambition, Achievement, Mark
Shocked	Surprised, Stunned, Agape, Stricken, Amazed, Frozen, Confounded, Dumbfounded, Loss for Words, At a loss, Flabbergasted, Aghast, Dismayed, Overwhelmed, Thunderstruck, Jolted
Believe	Belief, Conviction, Accept what being Said, Certain, Trust, To have faith in

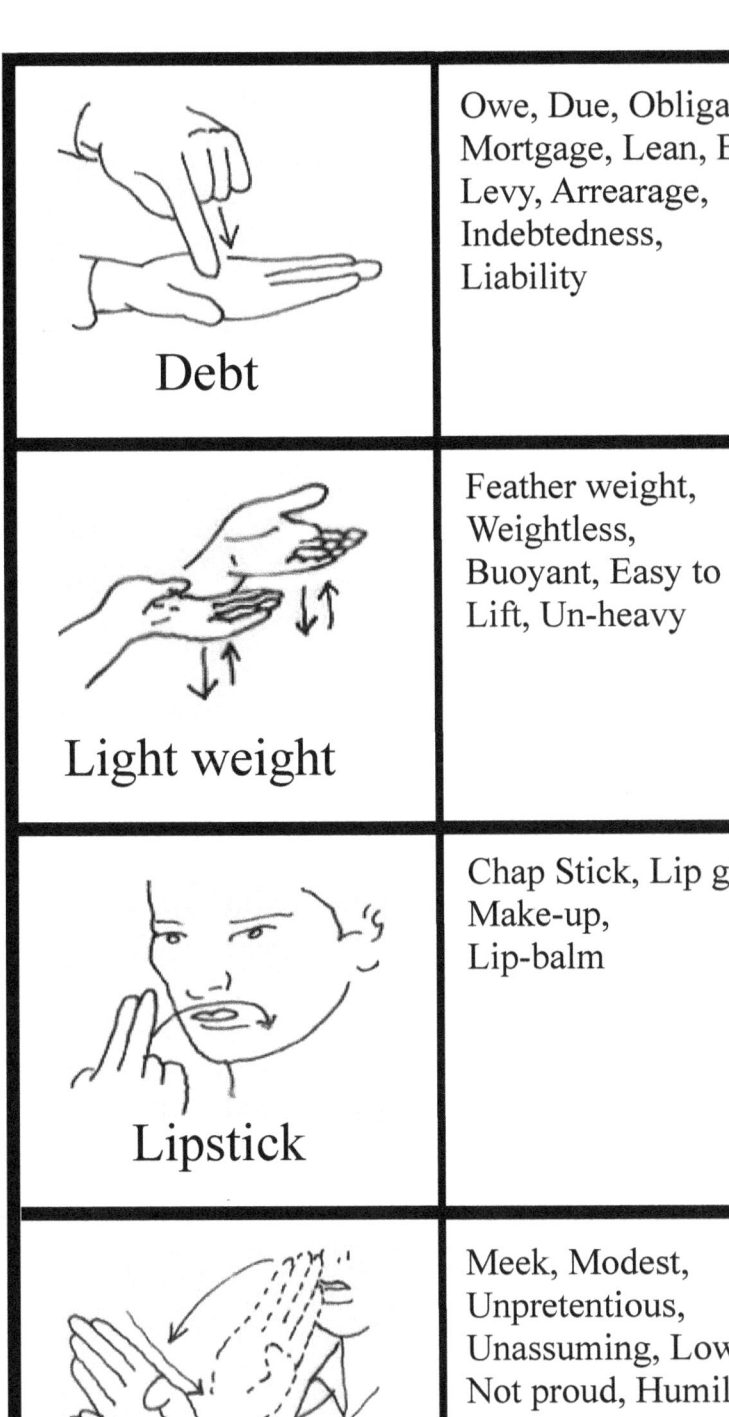

Debt	Owe, Due, Obligate, Mortgage, Lean, Bill, Levy, Arrearage, Indebtedness, Liability
Light weight	Feather weight, Weightless, Buoyant, Easy to Lift, Un-heavy
Lipstick	Chap Stick, Lip gloss, Make-up, Lip-balm
Humble	Meek, Modest, Unpretentious, Unassuming, Lowly, Not proud, Humility

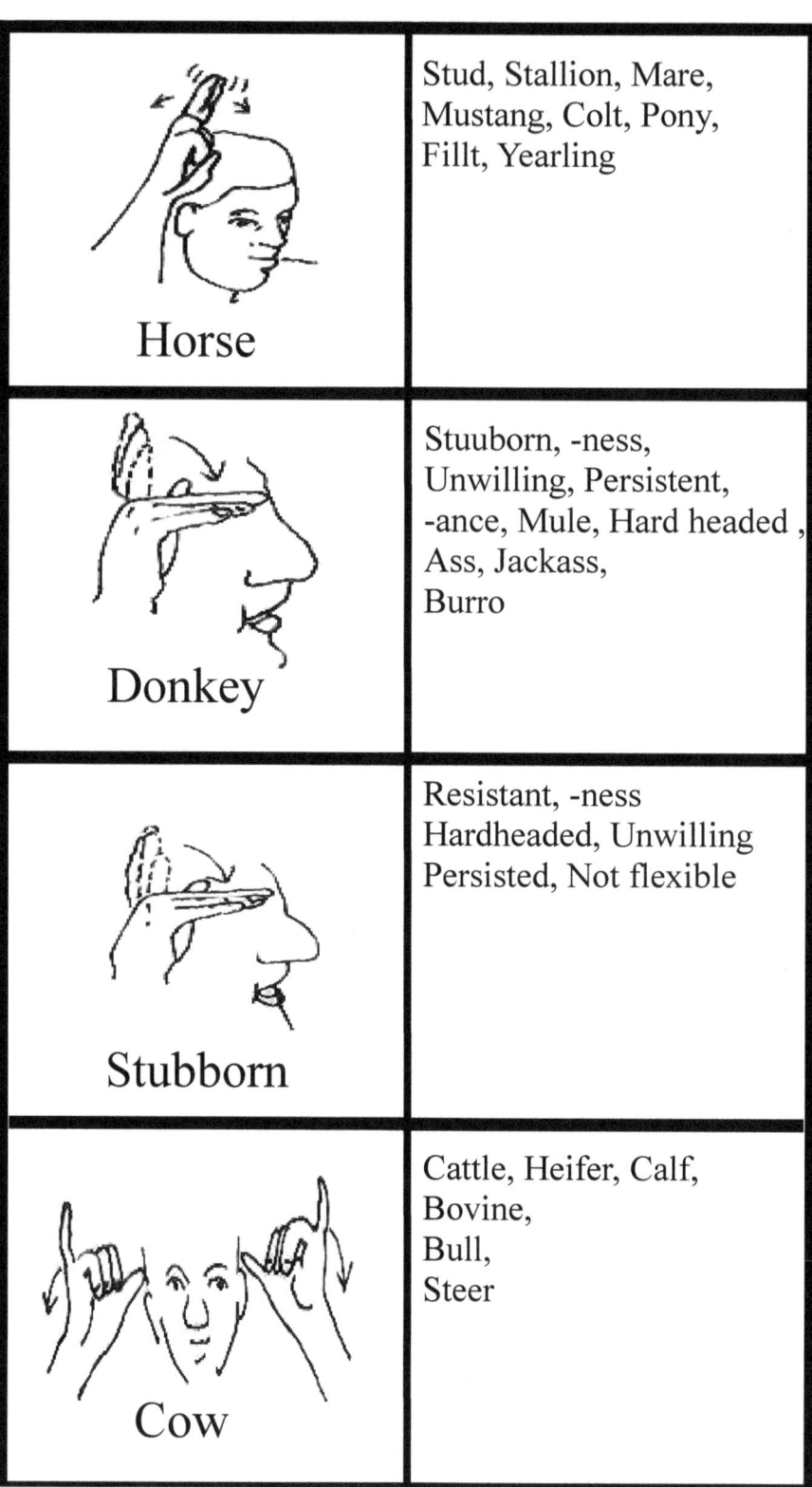

Horse	Stud, Stallion, Mare, Mustang, Colt, Pony, Fillt, Yearling
Donkey	Stuuborn, -ness, Unwilling, Persistent, -ance, Mule, Hard headed, Ass, Jackass, Burro
Stubborn	Resistant, -ness Hardheaded, Unwilling Persisted, Not flexible
Cow	Cattle, Heifer, Calf, Bovine, Bull, Steer

Idea	Clue, A thought, Inspiration, Notion, Precept, Suggestion
Imagination	Creative idea, Conceive, Fantasy, Make-up, Dream-up, Make, Believe, Think-up, Inspiration, Invention, Envision
Faith	Confidence, Trust, Reliance, Expectation, Belief
Trust	Confidence, Depend, Belief, Rely, Trustworthy

	Mischievous, Wicked, Devilish, Satan, Darkness, Dark side, Satanic, Lucifer, Beelzebub, Leviathan
Evil, Devil	
	Envy, Green'eyed, Covetous, Resentful, Desirous, Invidious
Jealous	
	Enemy, Contrary, Disagree, Against, Contrast, Enmity, Opposite
Oppose	
	Opposition, Competition, Opponent, Adversary, Foe, Rival
Enemy	

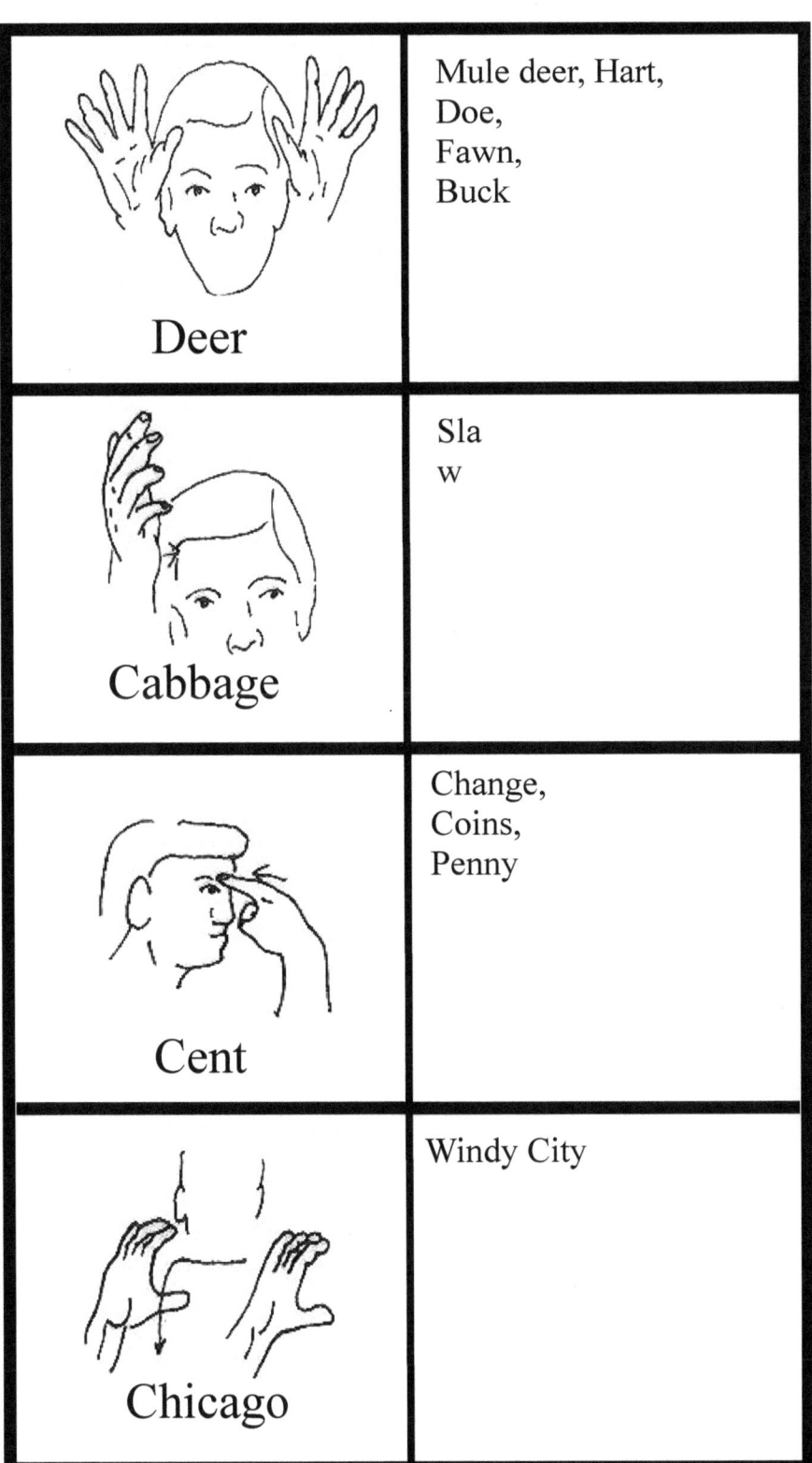

Deer	Mule deer, Hart, Doe, Fawn, Buck
Cabbage	Sla w
Cent	Change, Coins, Penny
Chicago	Windy City

Honor	Integrity, Esteem, Acknowledgement, Recognize, Look-up-to, Admire, Reverence, Elevate
Respect	Considerate, Esteem, Courtesy, Reverence, Admire, Deference, Revere, Think a lot of, Have high opinion of, Look up to, Show Consideration for
Understand	To know, Comprehend, Grasp, Discern, Acknowledge, Attain, Apprehend, Perceive, Savvy
Wise	Wisdom, Shrewd, Intelligent, Astute, Clver, Prudent, Sensible, Judicious

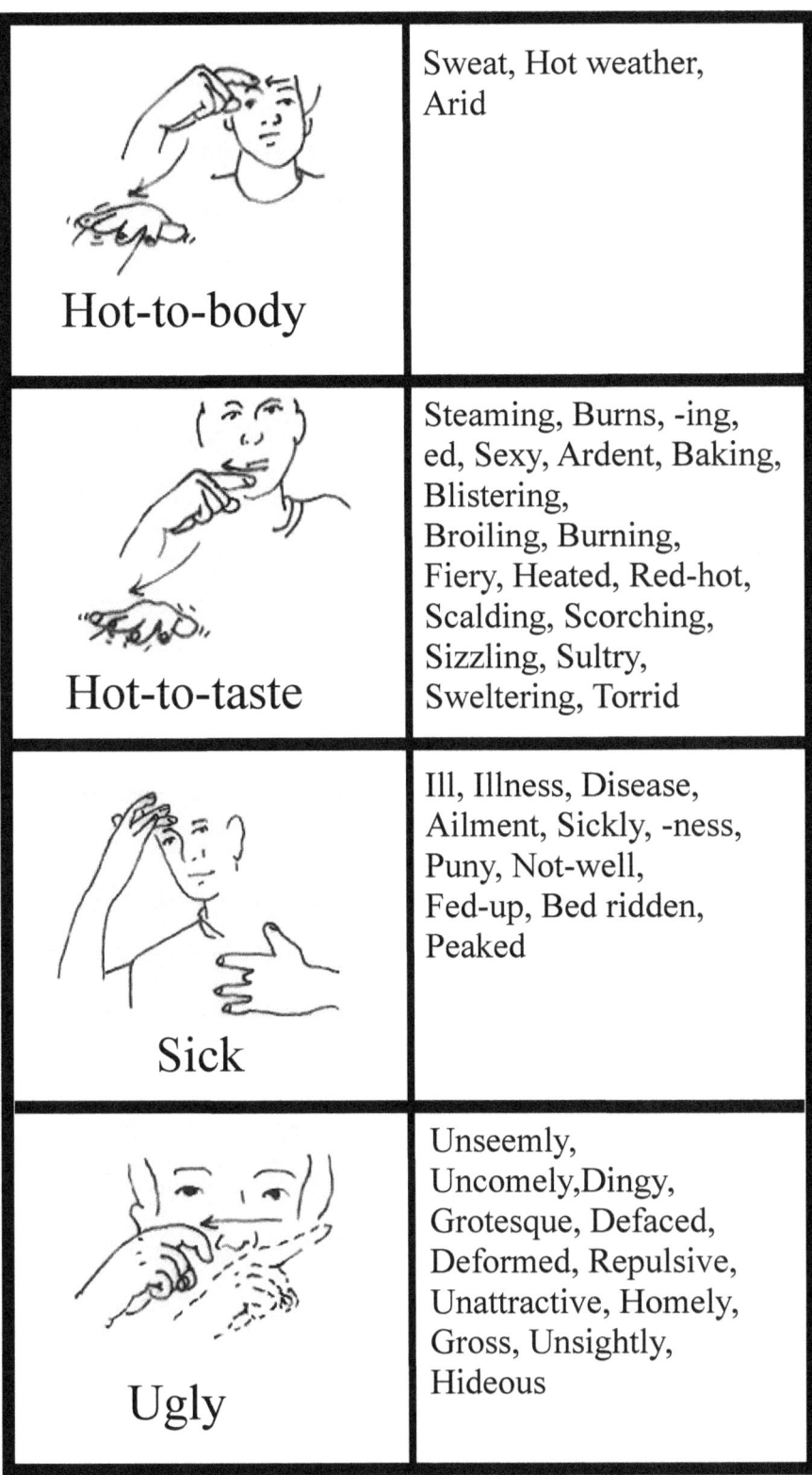

Hot-to-body	Sweat, Hot weather, Arid
Hot-to-taste	Steaming, Burns, -ing, ed, Sexy, Ardent, Baking, Blistering, Broiling, Burning, Fiery, Heated, Red-hot, Scalding, Scorching, Sizzling, Sultry, Sweltering, Torrid
Sick	Ill, Illness, Disease, Ailment, Sickly, -ness, Puny, Not-well, Fed-up, Bed ridden, Peaked
Ugly	Unseemly, Uncomely, Dingy, Grotesque, Defaced, Deformed, Repulsive, Unattractive, Homely, Gross, Unsightly, Hideous

Smell	Scent, Fume, Sniff, Fragrance, Aroma, Odor, Inhaled, Reek, Stench, -ed, -s
Flower	Blossom, Bloom, Bud
Bird	Beak, Robin, Chicken, Fowl, Pigeon, Fowl, Chirp
Elephant	Packaderm

Reason	Rationalize, Realize, -zation, Cause, Consider, Judgment, Mediate
Awful	Terrible, Horrible, Gross, Lousy, Disgusting, Dreadful, Yuck, Tragedy, -gic, Disastrous, Distasteful
Hat	Sun visor, Derby, Baseball cap, Sombrero, Helmet, Chappell
Summer	Hot

Wolf	Womanizer
Fox	Cunning, Sneaky, Sexy woman
Mouse	Vermin, Rodent, Mice, Weak Person
Rat	Rodent, Vermin, Bad Person

 Stuck up	Snob, -bby, bbish, Arrogant, Snooty, Haughty, Proud, Posh, Sophisticated, Conceited, Cavalier, Disdainful, High&Mighty, Huffy, Lofty, Overbearing, Pour hearted, Supercilious
 Fun	Humorous, Comical, Silly, Hilarious, Laughable, Entertaining, Droll, Hysterical, Clown around, Farcical, Galactic, Ludicrous, Ridiculous, Banter, Jest, Odd
 Stink	Putrid, Foul, Smelly, Funk, Reek, Stench
 Nosey	Busy body, Snoop, -py, Over involved, Butt-in, Interfere, Meddle, -ing, Gossip, Metal, Snoopy

Doll	Little girl, Stuffed Animal, Toy, Action figure, baby doll
Kid	Children, Offspring, Child, youngster, -guns, Juveniles, Moppets, Youth, Young ones
Napkin	Towel, Rag, Paper towel, Kleenex, Tissue, Handkerchief
Water	H2O

Bore	Uninteresting, Dry, Dull, Lack of interest, Undesirable, Palled, Tired, Wearied
Don't care	Unconcerned, Disinterested, Indifferent, Nonchalant, Apathetic, -thy, Don't mind
Lousy	Pathetic, Displeased, Terrible, Rotten, Spoiled, Un-tasteful, Unsatisfactory, Louse
Interesting	Like, Intriguing, Appealing, Attracting, Exciting, Fascinating, Captivating, Interested, Infatuating

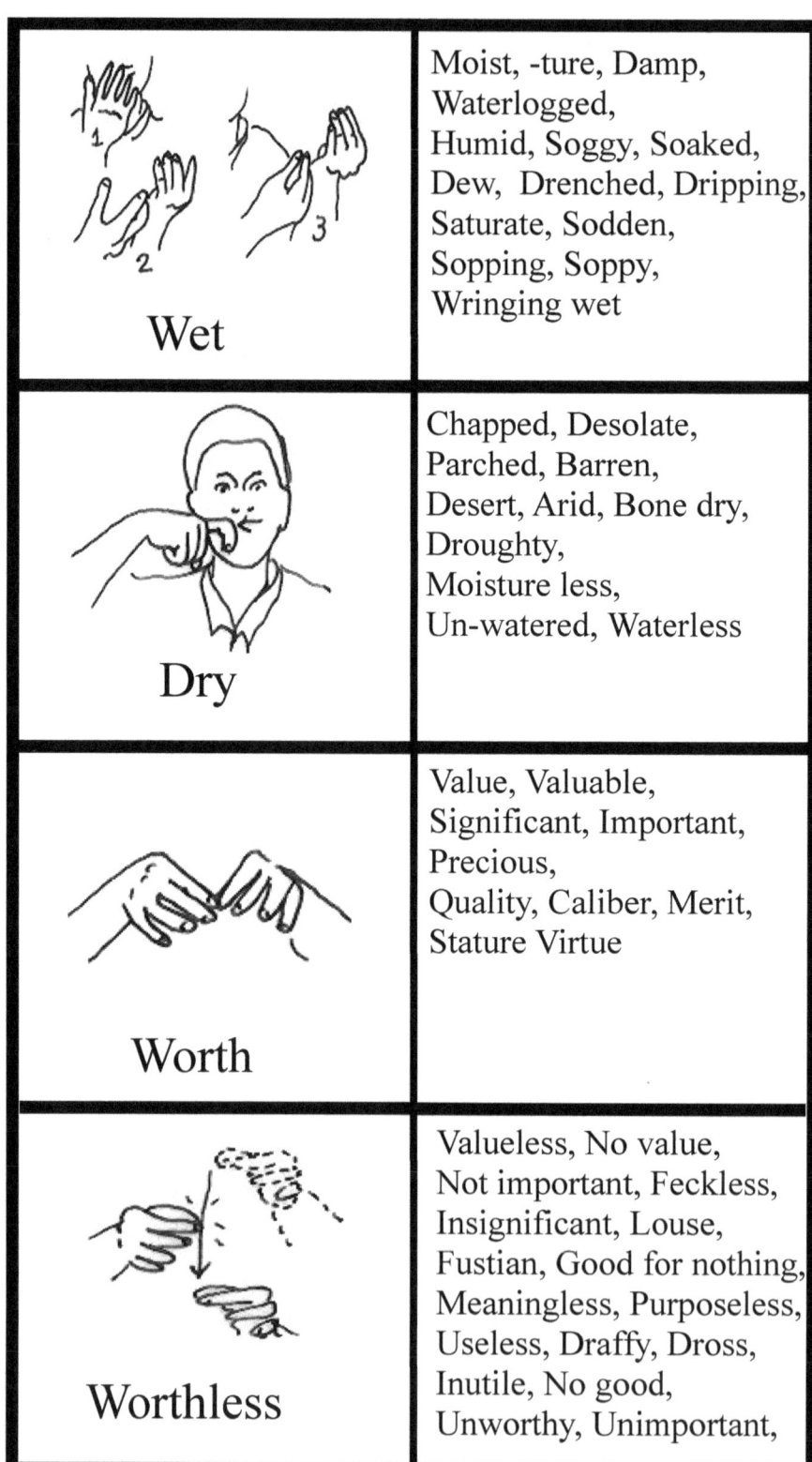

Wet	Moist, -ture, Damp, Waterlogged, Humid, Soggy, Soaked, Dew, Drenched, Dripping, Saturate, Sodden, Sopping, Soppy, Wringing wet
Dry	Chapped, Desolate, Parched, Barren, Desert, Arid, Bone dry, Droughty, Moisture less, Un-watered, Waterless
Worth	Value, Valuable, Significant, Important, Precious, Quality, Caliber, Merit, Stature Virtue
Worthless	Valueless, No value, Not important, Feckless, Insignificant, Louse, Fustian, Good for nothing, Meaningless, Purposeless, Useless, Draffy, Dross, Inutile, No good, Unworthy, Unimportant,

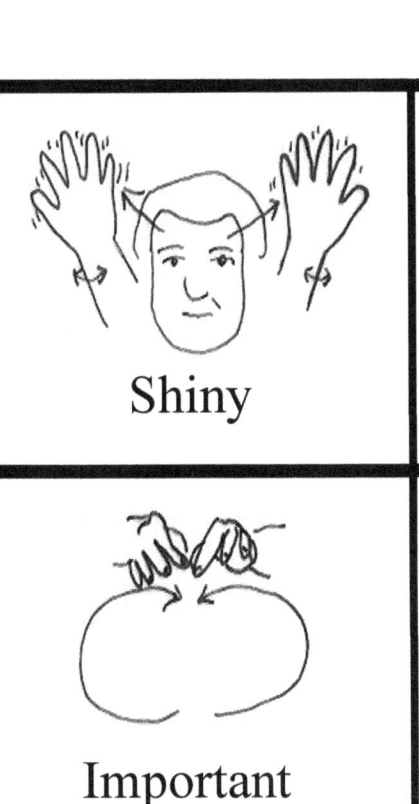 **Shiny**	Sparkling, -s, -ed, Twinkle, -ly, -ed, -ing, Glisten, Glitter, Glory, Bright, Glow, Dazzling, Lustrous, Burnished, Gleaming, Glistening, Glossy, Polished, Sheen, Shining
 **Important**	Worth, -y, Priority, Significant, -ed, -able, -ing, Crucial, Essential, Imperative, Vital, Meaningful, Momentous, Substantial
Connect	Belong, Join, Attach, Link, Unite, -ty, -ted, Combine, -ed, -ing, Hookup, Pinned, Fuse, Relationship, Chain, Associate, Coalesce, Coordinate, Connect, Couple, Link, Relate, Wed, Yoke
Analysis	Inspect, -ing, -ed, Critic, Diagnose, Dissect, -ing, -ed, Examination, Check over, Check up, Audit Review, Scan, Scrutiny, Survey

Chain	Series, Necklace, Beads, Link
Story	Tale, Stories, Narrative, Parable, Fable, Sentence, Folklore, Narration, Yarn, Chronicle
Language	Sentence, Grammar, Statement, Phrase, Dialect, Idiom, Speech, Tongue, Vernacular
Any	Whatever, Whoever, Whosoever, Anybody

Interpret	Translate, Explain, Construe, Explicate, Expound, Change
Court, Judge	Judicial system, Justice, Trail, Court house, Court room, Case, Hearing, Magistrate
Explain	Describe, Description, Define, -ing, -ed, -s, Expound, Give details, Construe, Explicate, Interpret, Spell out, Justify, Rationalize, Clarify, Clear up
Famliy	Relatives, Kin, Clan, Unit, Tribe, Domestic, Folks, Household, Kindred, Lineage, Stock

	Sight, Vision, Look, View
See	
Blind	Blinding, -ed, -ness, Sightless, Visually Impaired, Can't see, Overlook, Visionless
Look	Behold, Stare, Glaze, Spy, Survey, Observe, Appearance, Sight, Watch, Eye, Gape, Gaze, Goggle, Ogle
Watch	Observe, Spy, Probation, Stare, Look after, Survey, Gawk, Vigil, Vigilance, Mind, Tend, Attend

	Chive
Onion	
Silly	Goofy, Comical, Absurd, Foolish, Ridiculous, wacky, Stupid, Nonsense, Insane Giddy, Crazy, Bird witted, Harebrained, Idle headed,, Loopy, Loony, Preposterous, Tomfoolery, Featherbrained, Flighty, Rattle brained, Witless, Senseless, Scatterbrained
Foolish	Fool, Silly, Absurd, Ridicules, Unwise, Wrong decision, Worthless, Insane, Witless, Mindless, Nitwitted, Asinine
Clown	Jokester, Trickster, Comedian, Buffoon, Jester, Bozo, Funny, Person, Zany, Cutup, Farceur, Joker

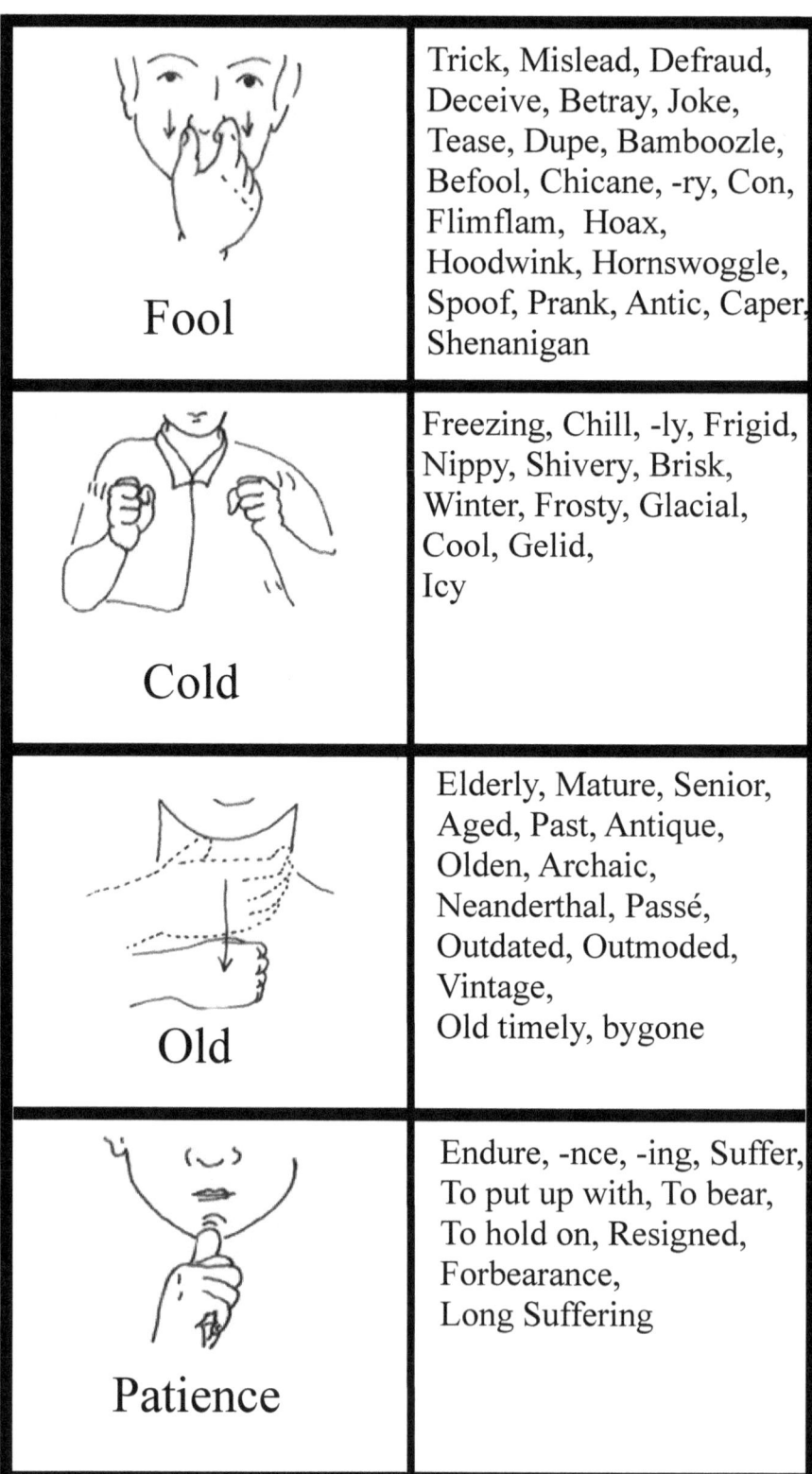

Fool	Trick, Mislead, Defraud, Deceive, Betray, Joke, Tease, Dupe, Bamboozle, Befool, Chicane, -ry, Con, Flimflam, Hoax, Hoodwink, Hornswoggle, Spoof, Prank, Antic, Caper, Shenanigan
Cold	Freezing, Chill, -ly, Frigid, Nippy, Shivery, Brisk, Winter, Frosty, Glacial, Cool, Gelid, Icy
Old	Elderly, Mature, Senior, Aged, Past, Antique, Olden, Archaic, Neanderthal, Passé, Outdated, Outmoded, Vintage, Old timely, bygone
Patience	Endure, -nce, -ing, Suffer, To put up with, To bear, To hold on, Resigned, Forbearance, Long Suffering

Seek	Search, Examine, Research, Hunt for, Look for, Pursue, Quest
Careless	Overlook, Inattentive, Reckless, Clumsy, Disheveled, Negligent Irresponsible, Feckless, Incautious, Un-careful, t, Lax,Un-thorough, Neglectful, Remiss, Slack, Slipshod, Sloppy, Ill kept, Thoughtless, Slovene,Heedless, Inadvertent, Unthinking Carelessness
Strict	Harsh, Firm, Rigid, Stern, Bold, Mean, controlling, Hard, Precise, Draconian, Ironhanded, Rigorist, Rigorous, Stringent, Un-permissive
Eye	Observe, Optic, Cornea, Ocular, Oculus, Peeper, Winker

Not	Ain't, Won't, Don't, Didn't, Doesn't, No way, Negative, Deny, Isn't
Nut	Kinds of nuts
Popsicle	Ice cream, Push up
Beer	Alcoholic beverage, Suds, Hops, Malt, Brew sky, Ale, Brew

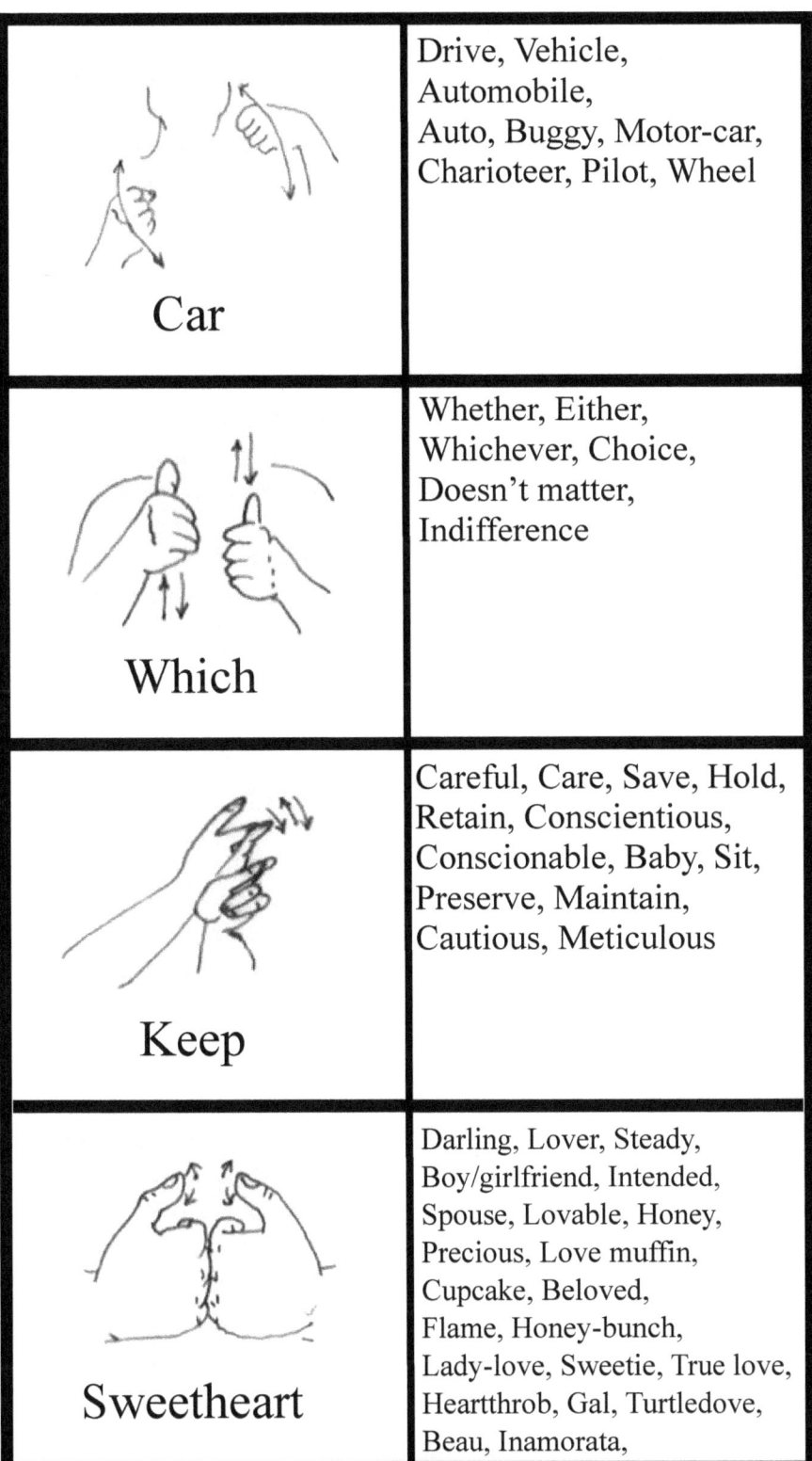

Car	Drive, Vehicle, Automobile, Auto, Buggy, Motor-car, Charioteer, Pilot, Wheel
Which	Whether, Either, Whichever, Choice, Doesn't matter, Indifference
Keep	Careful, Care, Save, Hold, Retain, Conscientious, Conscionable, Baby, Sit, Preserve, Maintain, Cautious, Meticulous
Sweetheart	Darling, Lover, Steady, Boy/girlfriend, Intended, Spouse, Lovable, Honey, Precious, Love muffin, Cupcake, Beloved, Flame, Honey-bunch, Lady-love, Sweetie, True love, Heartthrob, Gal, Turtledove, Beau, Inamorata,

Slave	Bondman, Bond-slave, Captive, Prisoner, Bond servant, Capture, Addict, Chattel
Get	Take, -ing, Acquire, -ing, Obtain, -ing, Annex, Gain, Landed, Procure
Strong	Strength, Mighty, Brave, Secure, Sure, Muscular, Firm, Fast, Stable, Staunch, Wieldy
Reserve	Save, Hold, Make Appointment, Reservation, Set Aside, Keep, Withhold, Retain

	Mistake, Error, Corrupt, Inaccurate, Incorrect, Erroneous, -ly, Unjust, Counterfactual, Specious, Unsound, Untrue, Misguided
Wrong	
	Tell, Talk, Told, Speak, Declare, Recite, Articulate, Enunciate, Phonate, Pronounce, State, Utter, Disclose, Divulge
Say	
	Note, Mail, Post card, Correspondence, Epistle, Missive
Letter	
	Phone, Call up, Receiver
Telephone	

Follow	Pursue, Stalk, Go after, Trail, Grasp meaning, Series, Sequel, Ensue, Succeed, Supervene, Comply, Conform, Observe Disciple
Break	Destroy, Snap, Fracture, Time out, Intermission, Recess, Smash, Damaged, Tear apart, Crack, Bust
Make	Create, Prepare, Construct, Produce, Mold, Compose, Formulate, Earn, Gain, Assemble, Construct, Originate
Baptize	Baptist, Submerge, Christen, Belief, Immersion

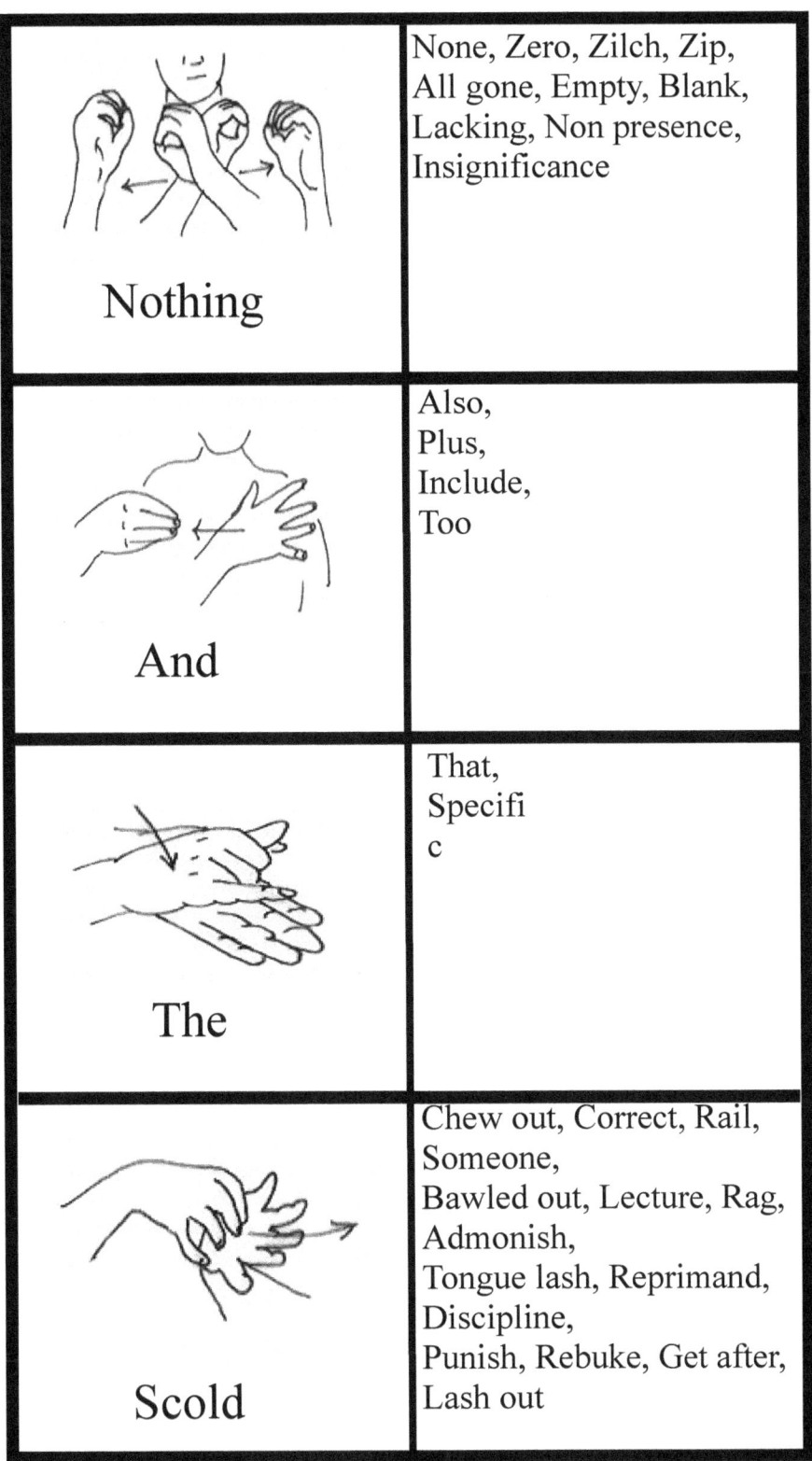

	None, Zero, Zilch, Zip, All gone, Empty, Blank, Lacking, Non presence, Insignificance
Nothing	
	Also, Plus, Include, Too
And	
	That, Specifi c
The	
	Chew out, Correct, Rail, Someone, Bawled out, Lecture, Rag, Admonish, Tongue lash, Reprimand, Discipline, Punish, Rebuke, Get after, Lash out
Scold	

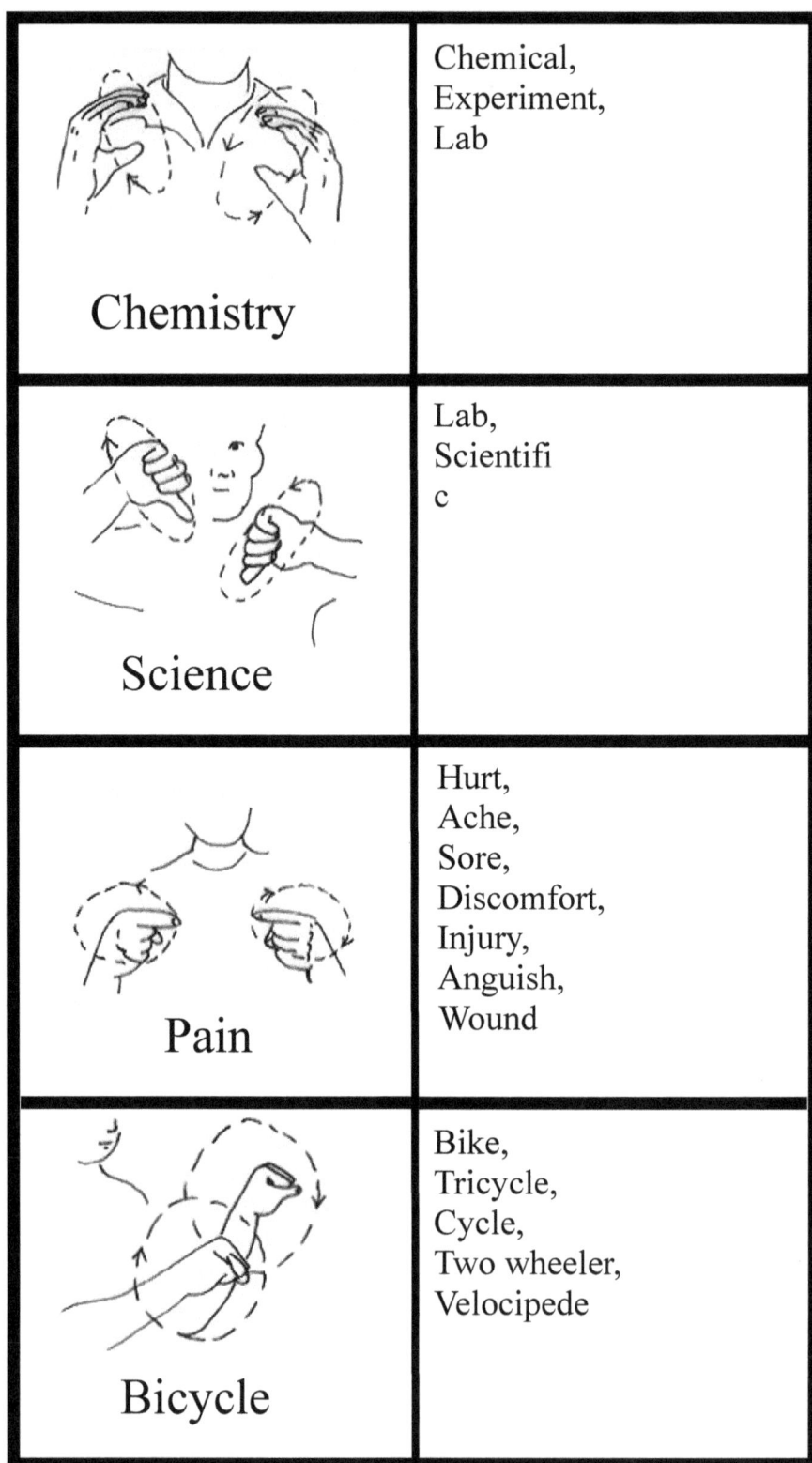

Chemistry	Chemical, Experiment, Lab
Science	Lab, Scientific
Pain	Hurt, Ache, Sore, Discomfort, Injury, Anguish, Wound
Bicycle	Bike, Tricycle, Cycle, Two wheeler, Velocipede

	Smooching, Romance, Kissing, Make-ing out
Necking	
Germany	German
Many	Abundance, A lot of, Lots, Numerous, Bunch, Multiple, Quantity, How mush, Plenty, Multitude, Populous, Sundry Voluminous
No	Not so, Refuse, Negative, Refusal, Forget it

	Greater amount, Again
More	
	Wreck, Amash, Accident, Collision, Collide, Impact, Concussion, Jolt, Collapse, Pileup
Crash	
	Together, Accompany, Go with, Along, Escort, In the company of, Partner, By, Conjointly, Jointly, Mutually
With	
	Have not, None, Absence, Lack, -ing
Without	

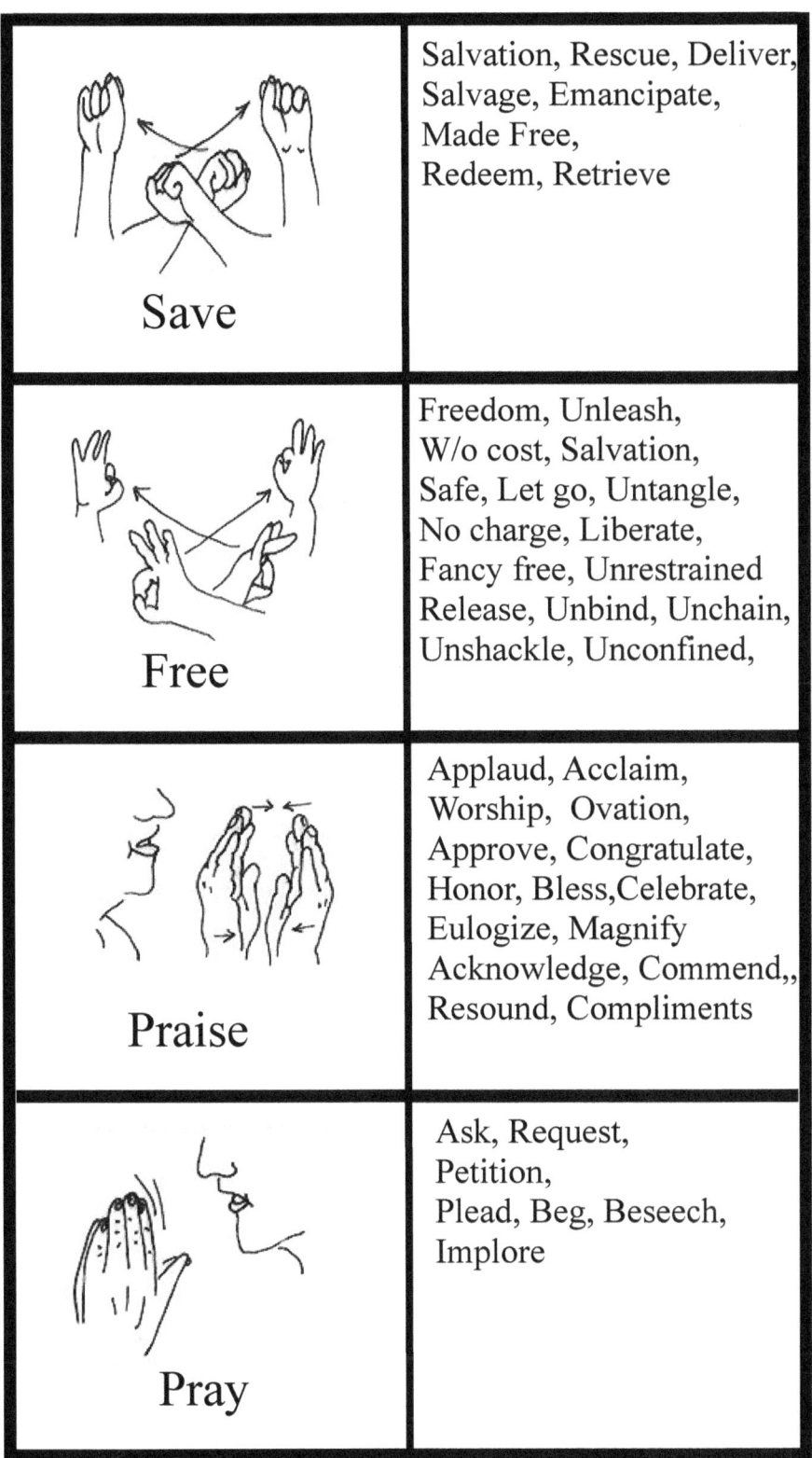

Save	Salvation, Rescue, Deliver, Salvage, Emancipate, Made Free, Redeem, Retrieve
Free	Freedom, Unleash, W/o cost, Salvation, Safe, Let go, Untangle, No charge, Liberate, Fancy free, Unrestrained Release, Unbind, Unchain, Unshackle, Unconfined,
Praise	Applaud, Acclaim, Worship, Ovation, Approve, Congratulate, Honor, Bless,Celebrate, Eulogize, Magnify Acknowledge, Commend,, Resound, Compliments
Pray	Ask, Request, Petition, Plead, Beg, Beseech, Implore

Use	Utilize, -zation, Consume, Exercise, Previously owned, 2nd hand
Question	Petition, Ask, Interrogate, Request, Inquire, Quiz, Imply, Remonstrance, Interrogation
God	Supreme being, Creator, Heavenly Father, Lord, Allah, Higher power, Jehovah
Never	Not, Not at all, Not ever, Nevermore

Shoe	Foot wear, Clogs, Sneakers, Tennis
Control	Administer, Conduct, Manage, Govern, Direct, Regulate, Rule, Control, -lled, -ing, Run, Discipline, Operate, Subdue, Handle, Dominate, Reign, Manage,
Fight	Battle, Conflict, Squall, Boxing, Fought, Quarrel, Hit, Punch, Rumble, Tiff, Squabble, Brawl, Altercation, Falling out, Controversy, Feud, Duel, Dispute, Run in, Knock-down-drag-out
Guard	Protect, Defend, Shield, Watch out for, Shelter, Security, Cover, Fend, Shield, Safeguard, Protection, Look out

Much	A Lot, Abundance, Great, Plenty, Large, Enormous, Great deal, Mass, Huge
Big	Large, Great, Huge, Enormous, Gigantic, gargantuan, Major, Exuberant, Sizeable, Large scale, Hefty
Small	Little, Tiny, Micro, Mini, Minuscule, Microscopic, Dinky, Lesser, Small fry, Small time, Measly Slight
Short	Brief, Moment, Fleeting, Soon, Quick, Skimpy, Snippy, Short and sweet

	Have to Have, Must have, Longing, Feel like, Crave, Desire, Wish
Want	
Beg	Plead, Grovel, Ask, Request, Implore, Solicit, Beseech, Appeal, Entreat, Supplicate, Grovel
Come	Approach, Invite, Appear, Move toward
Go	Went, Going, Will go, Leave, Depart, Go away, Go to, Exit, Take off, Run along

 Shower	Sprinkle, Baptize
 Grace	Unmerited favor
 Methodist	Sprinkle
 Light-to shine	Bright, -ten, Illuminate, Luminous, Illume, Lighten, Radiate

	Kids, Child, Youths, off-spring, Brood, Rug rats, Descendants, Posterity, Juveniles, Moppets, Young ones, Youngsters
Children	
	Canyon, Ravine, Gully, Dip
Vally	
	Invite, Hire, Employ
Welcome	
	Decease, -d, Pass away, Death, Lost, Late, Died, No longer living, Gone, Inanimate demise, Muted, Extinct, Corpse, Bygone, Departed, Lifeless, Deadened, Spiritless, Unfeeling,
Dead	

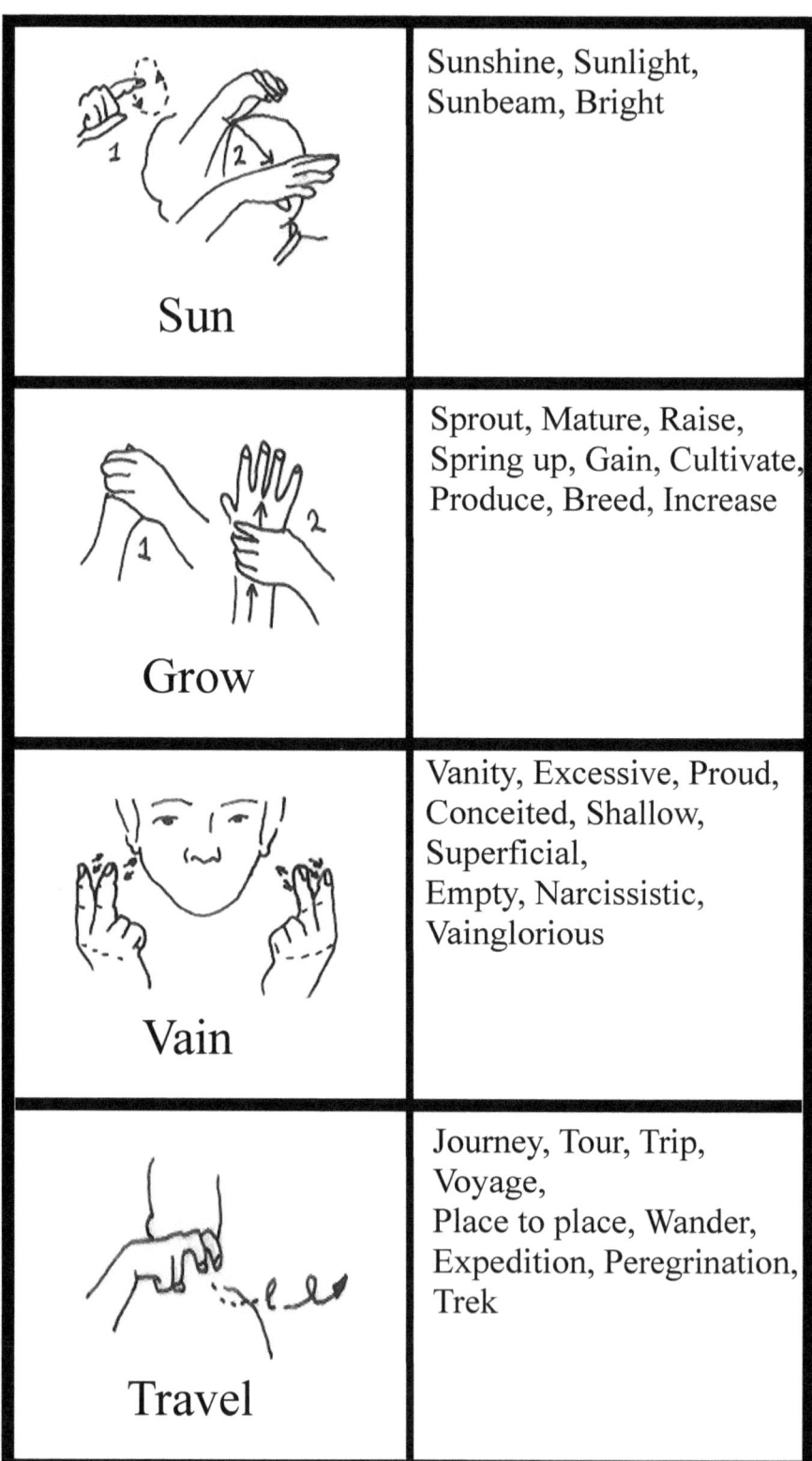

	Sunshine, Sunlight, Sunbeam, Bright
Sun	
	Sprout, Mature, Raise, Spring up, Gain, Cultivate, Produce, Breed, Increase
Grow	
	Vanity, Excessive, Proud, Conceited, Shallow, Superficial, Empty, Narcissistic, Vainglorious
Vain	
	Journey, Tour, Trip, Voyage, Place to place, Wander, Expedition, Peregrination, Trek
Travel	

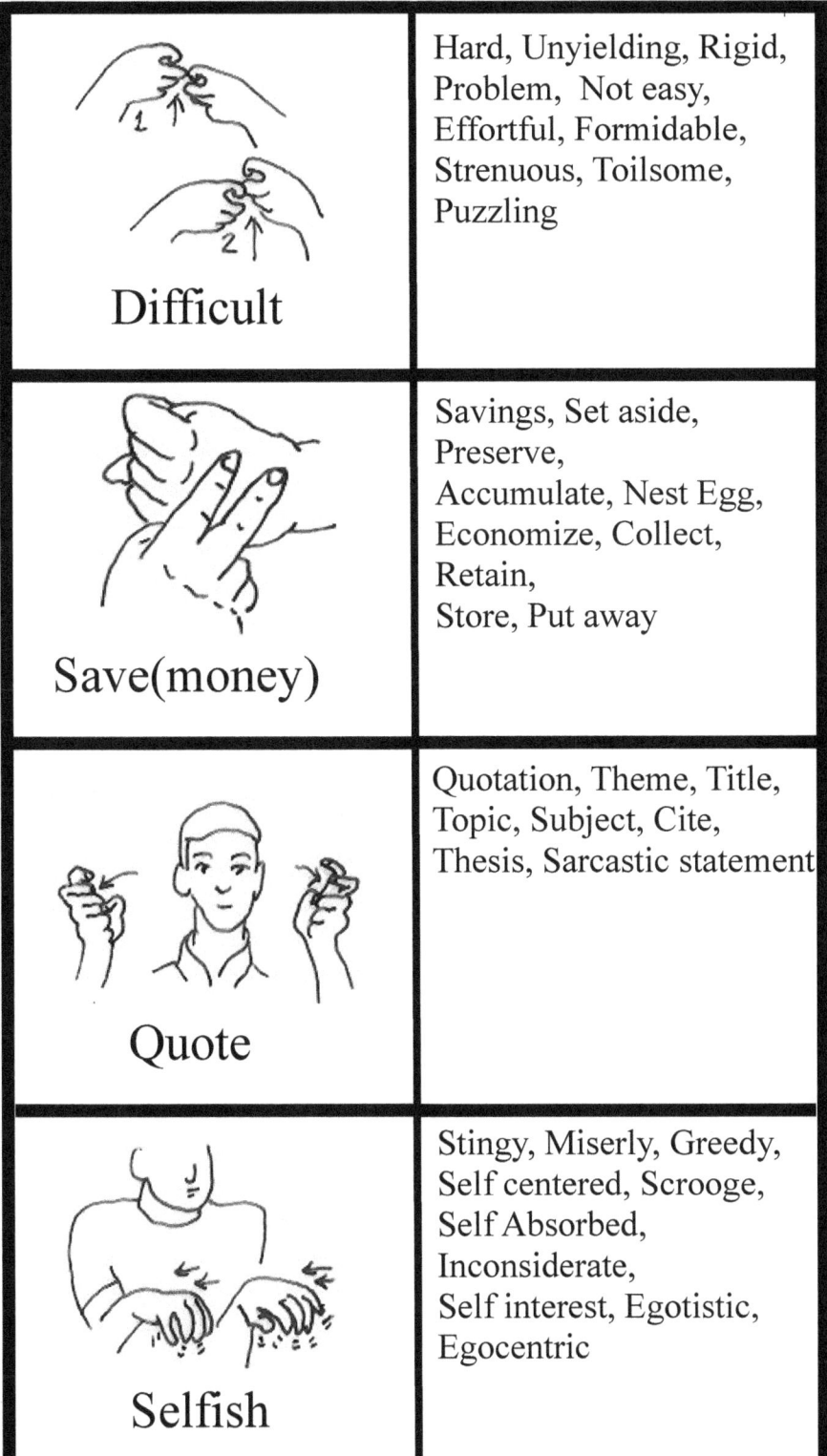

Difficult	Hard, Unyielding, Rigid, Problem, Not easy, Effortful, Formidable, Strenuous, Toilsome, Puzzling
Save(money)	Savings, Set aside, Preserve, Accumulate, Nest Egg, Economize, Collect, Retain, Store, Put away
Quote	Quotation, Theme, Title, Topic, Subject, Cite, Thesis, Sarcastic statement
Selfish	Stingy, Miserly, Greedy, Self centered, Scrooge, Self Absorbed, Inconsiderate, Self interest, Egotistic, Egocentric

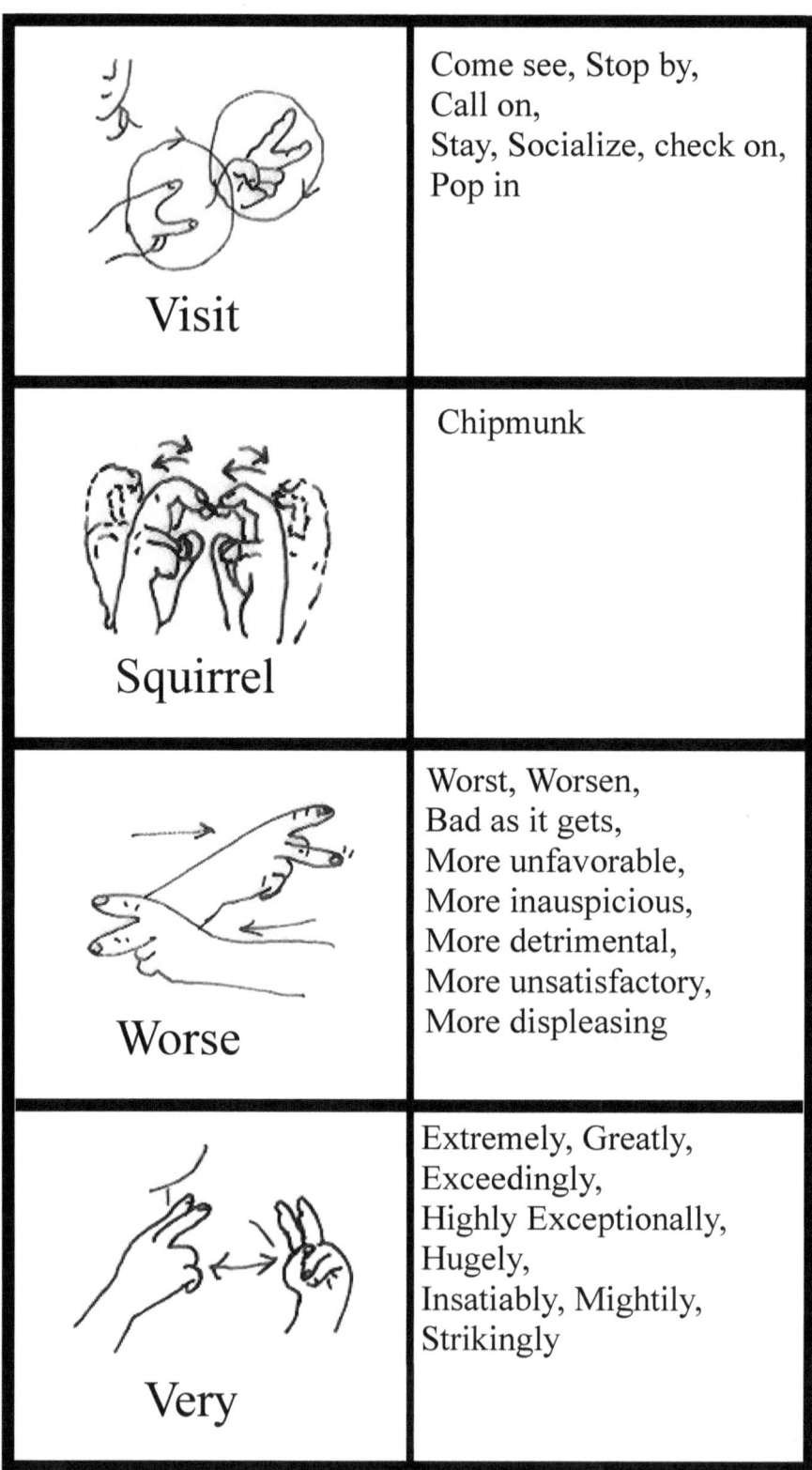

Visit	Come see, Stop by, Call on, Stay, Socialize, check on, Pop in
Squirrel	Chipmunk
Worse	Worst, Worsen, Bad as it gets, More unfavorable, More inauspicious, More detrimental, More unsatisfactory, More displeasing
Very	Extremely, Greatly, Exceedingly, Highly Exceptionally, Hugely, Insatiably, Mightily, Strikingly

 **Scissors**	Sheers, Trim, Cut, Edge, Clip, Clippers, Snipers
Virgin	Unspoiled, Untouched, Innocent, Pure, W/o alcohol, Virginity, Chaste, Unadulterated, Untapped
Tournament	Contest, Game, Competition, Playoff, Challenge
Hard	Difficult, Not easy, Complicated, Solid, Firm, Inflexible, Rigid, Complex, Tough, Effortful, Formidable, Strenuous

Sweet	Sweetener, Pleasure, Gentle, Agreeable, Amiable, Caring, Precious, Confection, Tender, Winsome
Cute	Good looking, Adorable, Handsome, Pleasing, Dainty
Good	Well done, Well Behaved, Virtuous, Well reputable, Upstanding, Skillful, Decorous
Bad	Wicked, Harmful, Evil, Nasty, Spoiled, Not good, Unfavorable, Naughty, Inaccurate, Mischievous, Ruined, Inauspicious, Ill behaved, Misbehaving, Immoral, Iniquitous, Reprobate, Sinful, Vicious

Bachelor	Single man, Unmarried male
Kiss	Smooch, Peck, Make out, Buss, Lip, Osculate, Smack
Homosexual	Gay, Same sex relationship, Queer, homoerotic, Homophile
Disappoint	Sour, Disillusioned, Disappointment, Unsatisfied

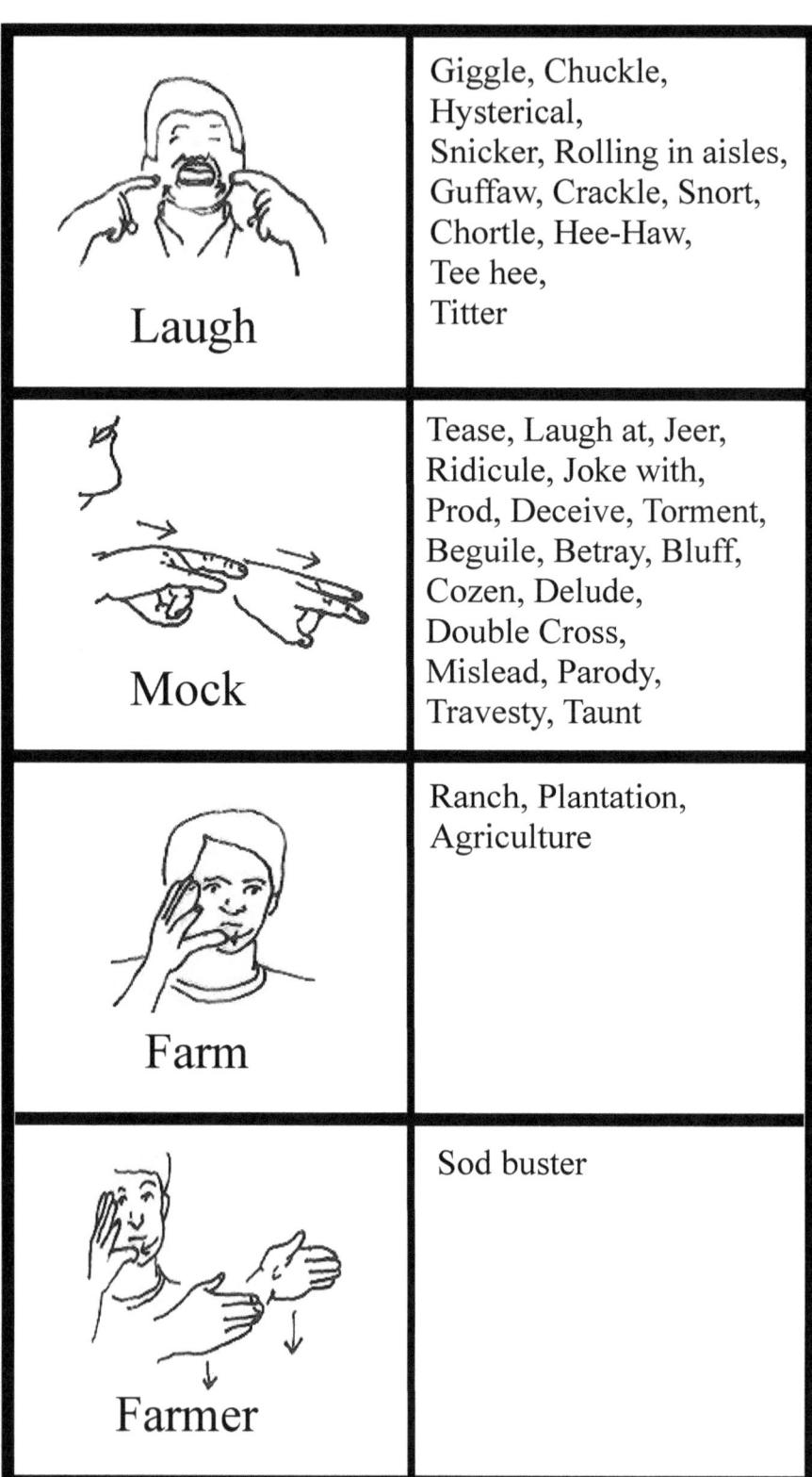

Laugh	Giggle, Chuckle, Hysterical, Snicker, Rolling in aisles, Guffaw, Crackle, Snort, Chortle, Hee-Haw, Tee hee, Titter
Mock	Tease, Laugh at, Jeer, Ridicule, Joke with, Prod, Deceive, Torment, Beguile, Betray, Bluff, Cozen, Delude, Double Cross, Mislead, Parody, Travesty, Taunt
Farm	Ranch, Plantation, Agriculture
Farmer	Sod buster

Thank you	Give thanks, Gratitude, Grateful, Appreciative, Thankful, Delighted, Obliged
Send	Mail, Transmit, Send off, Emit, Convey, Sending, Dispatch, Forward, Remit, Route, Ship
Dirty	Pig, Filthy, Swine, Dingy, Boar, Unclean, Grimy, Pornographic, Dungy, Not clean, Murky, Stain Obscene, Mucky, Nasty, Sloppy, Foul, Grubby, Sordid, Squalid, Immoral, Unchaste, Gross, Profane, Rank, Raunchy, Smutty, Vulgar, Tarnish, Smudge,
Elevator	Lift

Jew	Jewish, Hebrew, To conserve
Drool	Envy, Long for, Desire, Lust, Salivate, Slobber, Crave, Desiderate
Bitter	Disappointed, Distasteful, Galling, Grievous, Unpalatable, Acerb, Acrid, Disillusioned, Astringent, Austere, Acerbic, Tart, Acidulous, Acidic
Blood	Plasma, Bleeding, Hemoglobin

	Native American
Indian	
	Can't hear, Hearing Impaired
Deaf	
	Vow, Pact, Swear, Guarantee, Commit, Pledge, Oath, Omen, Portend, Presage
Promise	
	Prefer, Preference
Favorite	

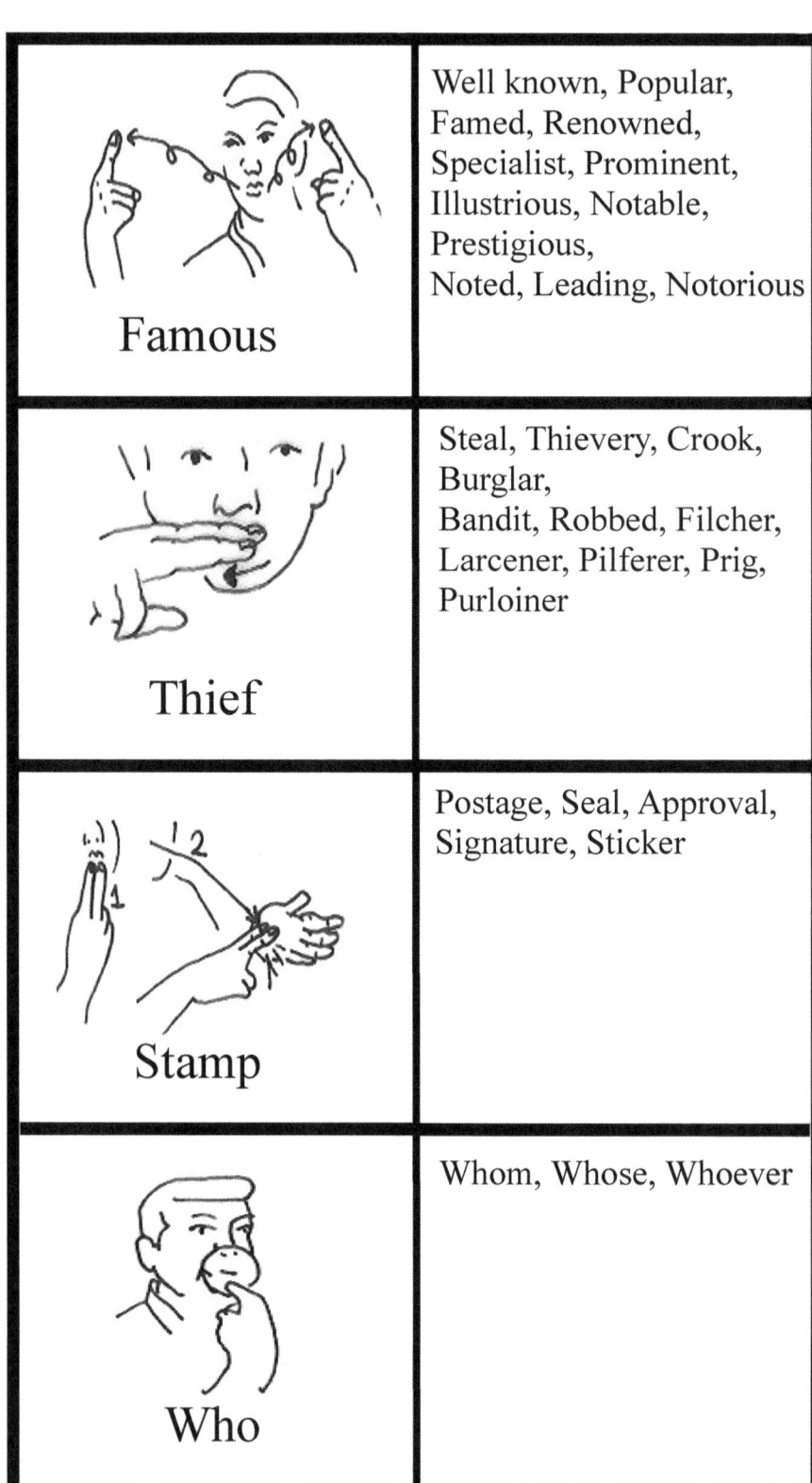

Famous	Well known, Popular, Famed, Renowned, Specialist, Prominent, Illustrious, Notable, Prestigious, Noted, Leading, Notorious
Thief	Steal, Thievery, Crook, Burglar, Bandit, Robbed, Filcher, Larcener, Pilferer, Prig, Purloiner
Stamp	Postage, Seal, Approval, Signature, Sticker
Who	Whom, Whose, Whoever

Tomato	'mater s
Syrup	Honey
Sure	True, -thful, -lly, Actually, Absolutely, Valid, Genuine, Really, Right, Loyal, Correct, Positive, Am, Is, Are, Was,, Been, Being, Infallible, Inerrable, Surefire, Inerrant, Unerring, Certain,Un-failing, Inarguable, Incontestable, Incontrovertible, Indisputable, ~~Undeniable, Confident, Were~~
Candy	Sweets, Cute, Sugar, Confection

Duck	Quack, Duckling, Mallard
Warm	Almost hot, Friendly, Likeable, Aglow
Eat	Food, Pig out, Ate, Consume, Devour, Ingest, Meal, Partake
Food	Eat, Meal, Consume, Edibles, Feed, Chow, Grub, Provisions, Victuals

Lip Reading	Oral, Speech reading
Hearing Aid	Listening aid
Wine	Liquor, Liquors
Taste	Kind, Prefer, -ences

	Savory, -ing, Palatable, Luscious, Appetizing, Real Good, Yummy, tasty, Scrumptious, Delightful
Delicious	
Everyday	Daily, Always, Common, Customary
Tobacco	Chewing, Pipe, Wad, Snuff
Dentist	Tooth Doctor, Gum, Doctor, Orthodontist

Orange (fruit)	Orange Juice, Orange Drink
Home	Abode, House, residence, Domicile, Habitat, Apartment, Shelter, Dwelling
Hungry	Starving, Ravenous, Famished, Voracious
Desire	Passion, Longing, Wanting, Yearning, Covet, Crave, Desiderate, Urge

Teeth	Glass, Enamel, Bone, Concrete
Embarrassed	Bashful, Humiliated, Ashamed, Warm, Flushed, Abashed
Shy	Bashful, Ashamed, Introvert, Demure, Meek, Timid, Coy, Diffident, Modest, Self effacing, Unassertive, Un-assured
Hear	Eaves drop, Noise, Attend, Hark, Hearken, Heed

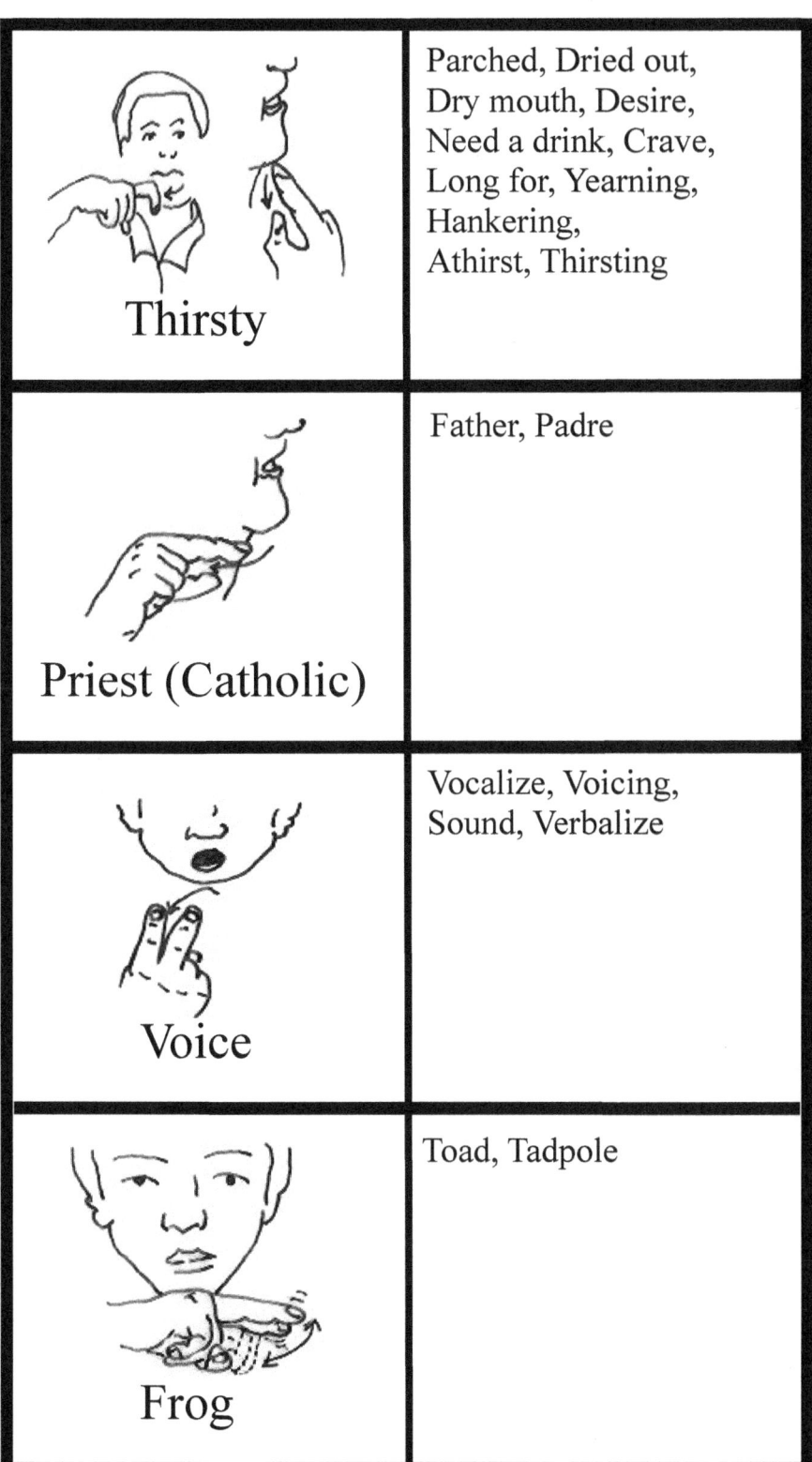

Thirsty	Parched, Dried out, Dry mouth, Desire, Need a drink, Crave, Long for, Yearning, Hankering, Athirst, Thirsting
Priest (Catholic)	Father, Padre
Voice	Vocalize, Voicing, Sound, Verbalize
Frog	Toad, Tadpole

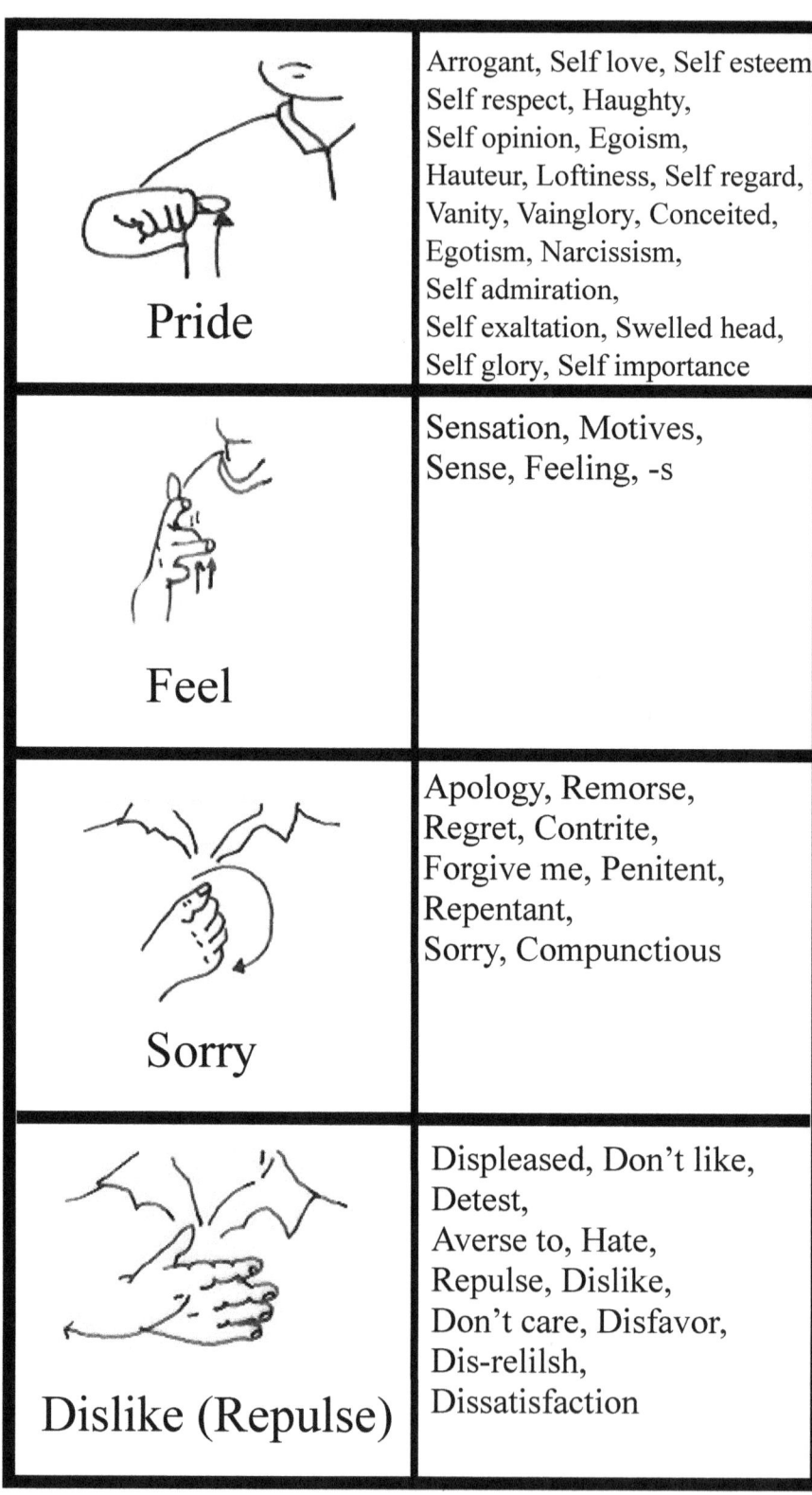

Pride	Arrogant, Self love, Self esteem Self respect, Haughty, Self opinion, Egoism, Hauteur, Loftiness, Self regard, Vanity, Vainglory, Conceited, Egotism, Narcissism, Self admiration, Self exaltation, Swelled head, Self glory, Self importance
Feel	Sensation, Motives, Sense, Feeling, -s
Sorry	Apology, Remorse, Regret, Contrite, Forgive me, Penitent, Repentant, Sorry, Compunctious
Dislike (Repulse)	Displeased, Don't like, Detest, Averse to, Hate, Repulse, Dislike, Don't care, Disfavor, Dis-relilsh, Dissatisfaction

Bee	Gnat
Gold	Golden, California
Secretary	Assistant, Office, Support, Take Minutes, Clerk, Record keeper, Receptionist
Gum	Chewing gum, Bubble gum

	Canadian, Canook
Canada	
	Tub, Bathe, Wash
Bath	
	Military, Soldier
Army	
	Puff up, Vaunt, Crow, Gasconade, Prate
Boast	

Please	Pleasure, Take joy in, Gratify, Pleasurable, Relish, Delight, Delectable, Gladden, Happily, Voluptuous
Our	Ours
Refuse	Won't, Reject, Resist, Decline, Reprobate, Withhold, Disallow, Keep back
Rebel	Rebellious, Revolt, Mutiny, Anarchist, Insurrect, malcontent, Mutineer, Rice against, Revolutionary

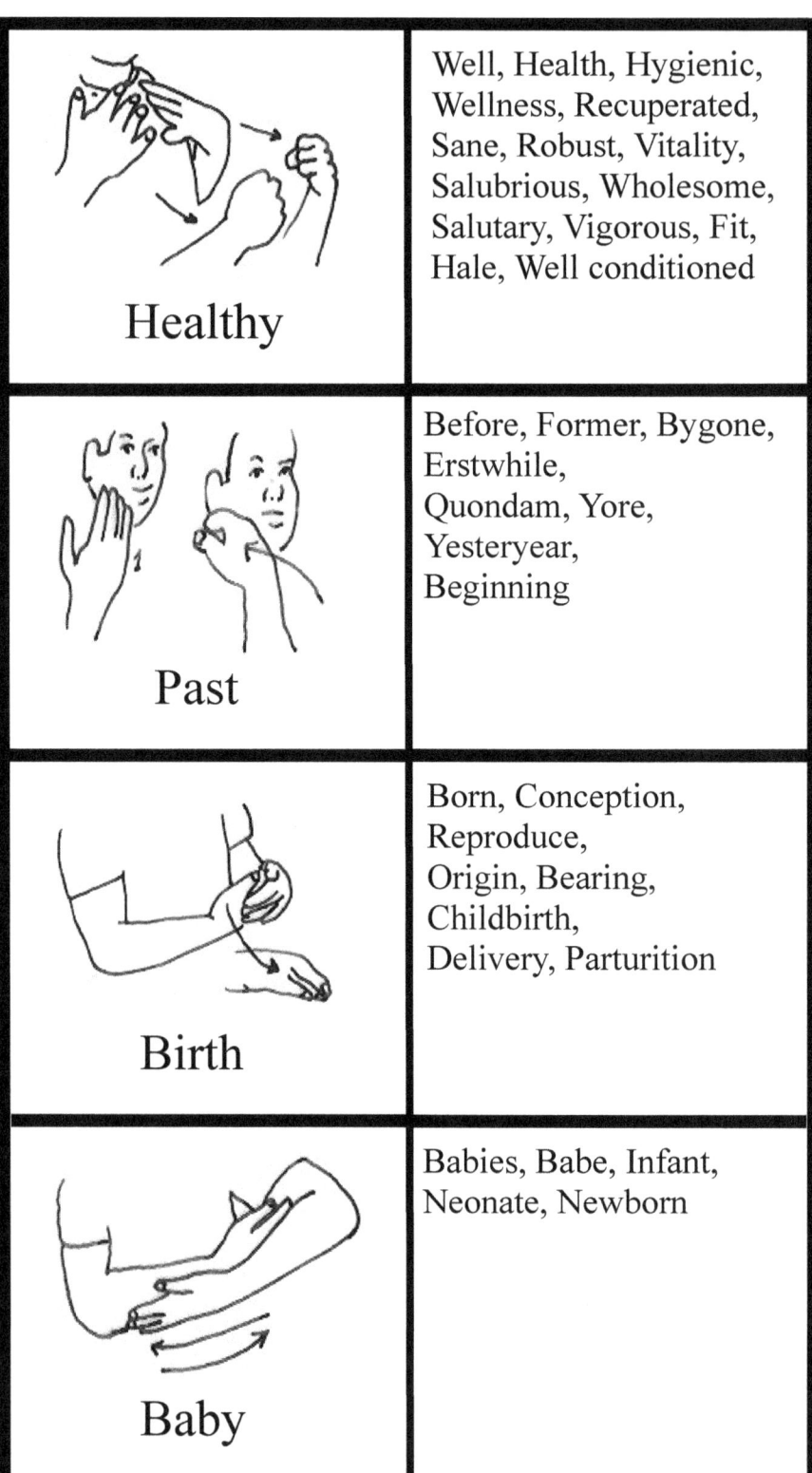

Healthy	Well, Health, Hygienic, Wellness, Recuperated, Sane, Robust, Vitality, Salubrious, Wholesome, Salutary, Vigorous, Fit, Hale, Well conditioned
Past	Before, Former, Bygone, Erstwhile, Quondam, Yore, Yesteryear, Beginning
Birth	Born, Conception, Reproduce, Origin, Bearing, Childbirth, Delivery, Parturition
Baby	Babies, Babe, Infant, Neonate, Newborn

Love	Adore, Cherish, To hold dear, Affection, Tender, Attachment, Devotion, Fondness, Amour, Passion
Happy	Glad, Exuberant, Joyful, Joyous, Lighthearted, Benevolent
Joy	Joyful, Glad, Pleasure, Delectation, Delight, Enjoyment, Fruition, Joyance
Like	Desire, Fancy, Enjoy, Relish, Interest

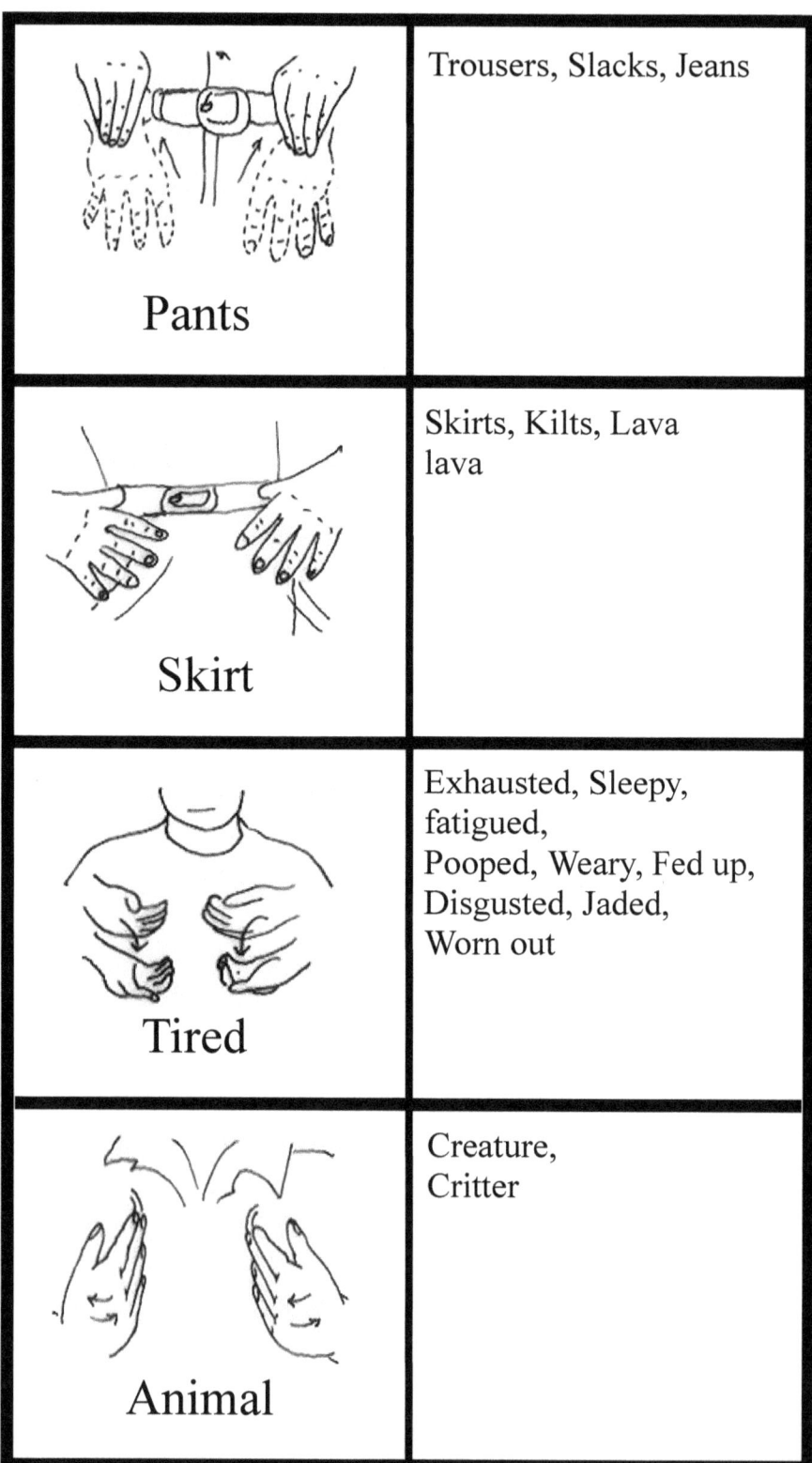

Pants	Trousers, Slacks, Jeans
Skirt	Skirts, Kilts, Lava lava
Tired	Exhausted, Sleepy, fatigued, Pooped, Weary, Fed up, Disgusted, Jaded, Worn out
Animal	Creature, Critter

Burden	Load, Weight, Charge, Deadweight, Duty, Millstone, Onus, Task, Tax, Encumber
Angel	Angels, Archangel, Celestial being, Heavenly being, Convince, Seraphim, cherubim, Cherub
Snow	Snowfall, Snowflake
Satisfied	Contented, Gratified, Appeased, Convinced, Filled, Fulfilled, Assured, Persuaded, Suited

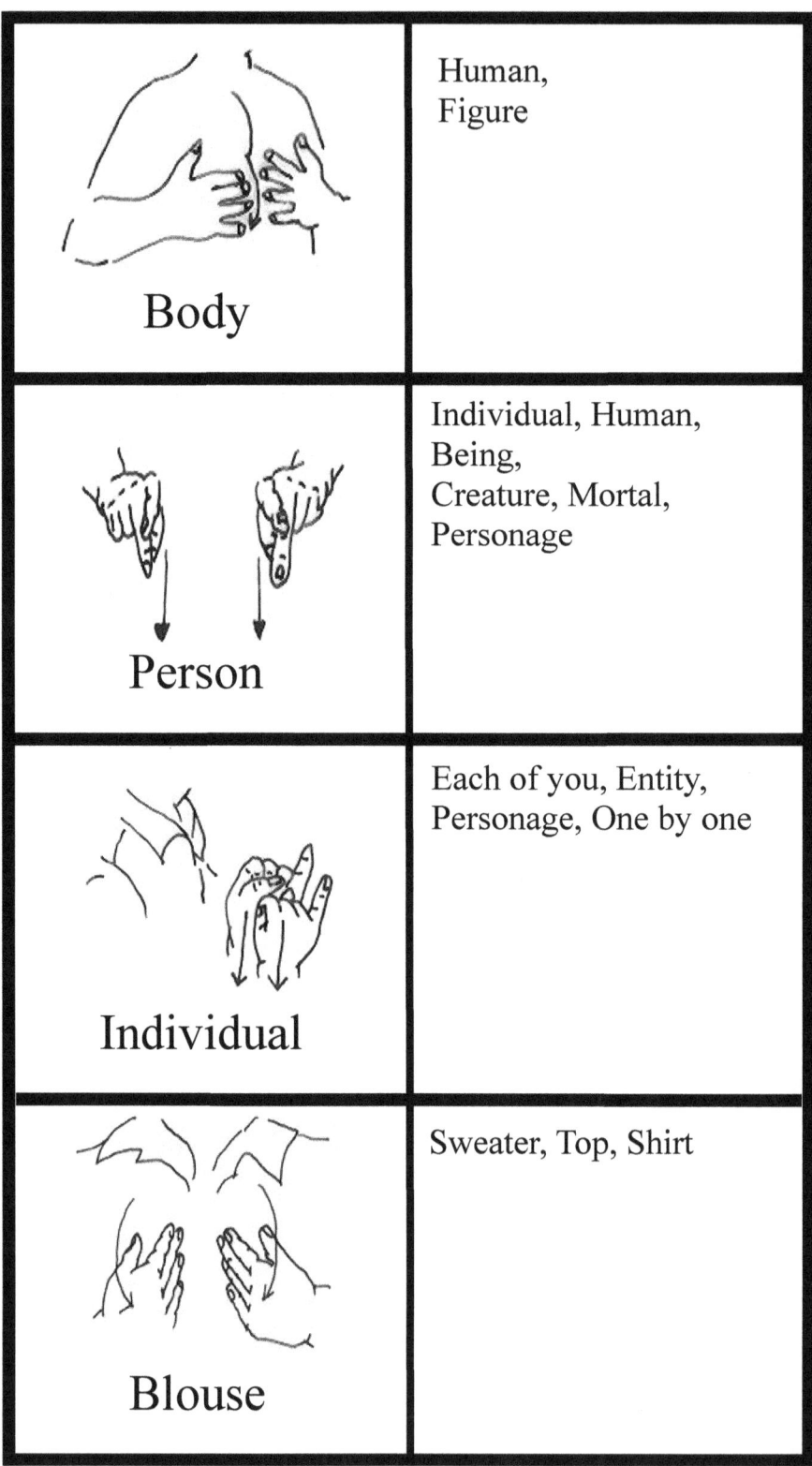

	Human, Figure
Body	
Person	Individual, Human, Being, Creature, Mortal, Personage
Individual	Each of you, Entity, Personage, One by one
Blouse	Sweater, Top, Shirt

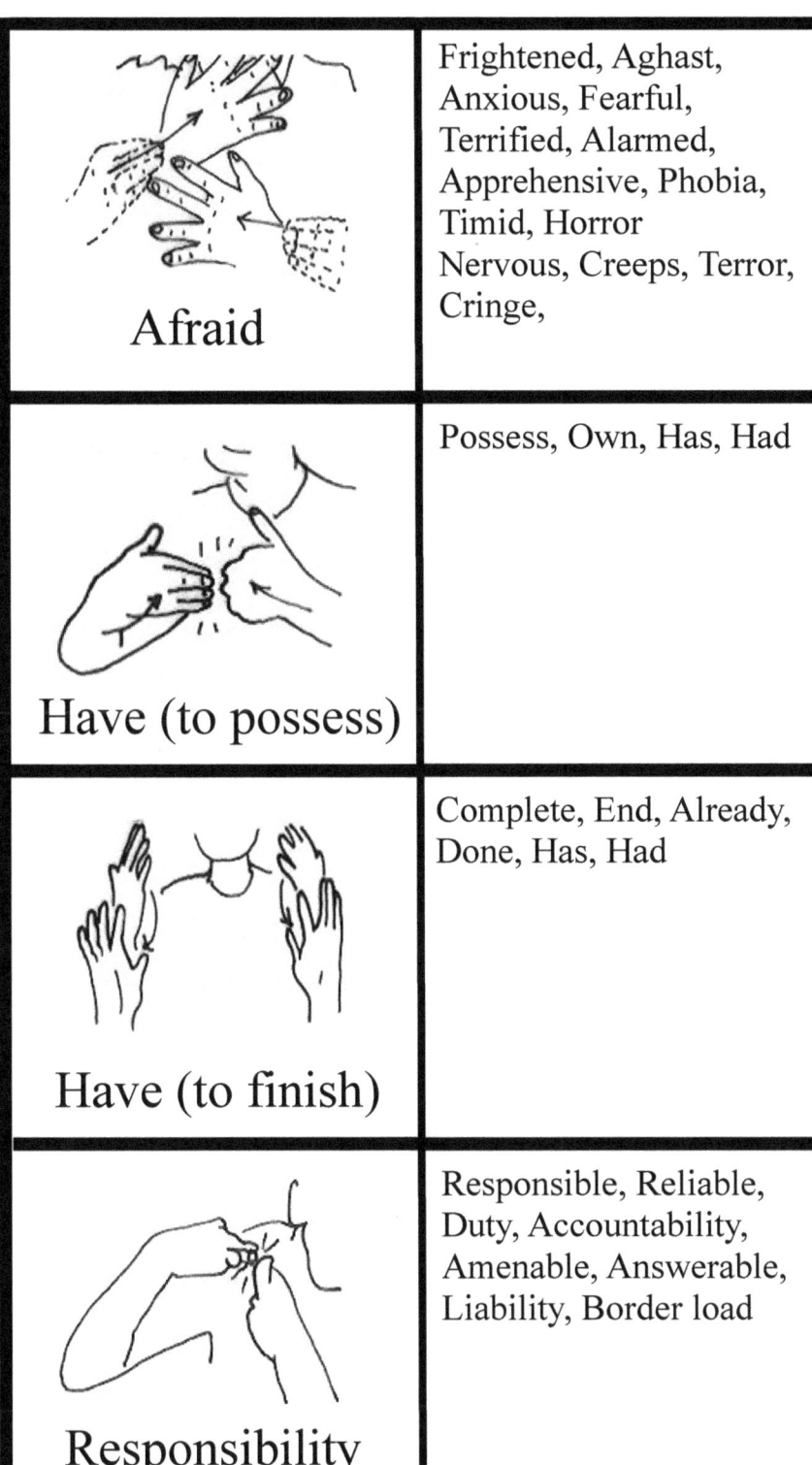

Afraid	Frightened, Aghast, Anxious, Fearful, Terrified, Alarmed, Apprehensive, Phobia, Timid, Horror Nervous, Creeps, Terror, Cringe,
Have (to possess)	Possess, Own, Has, Had
Have (to finish)	Complete, End, Already, Done, Has, Had
Responsibility	Responsible, Reliable, Duty, Accountability, Amenable, Answerable, Liability, Border load

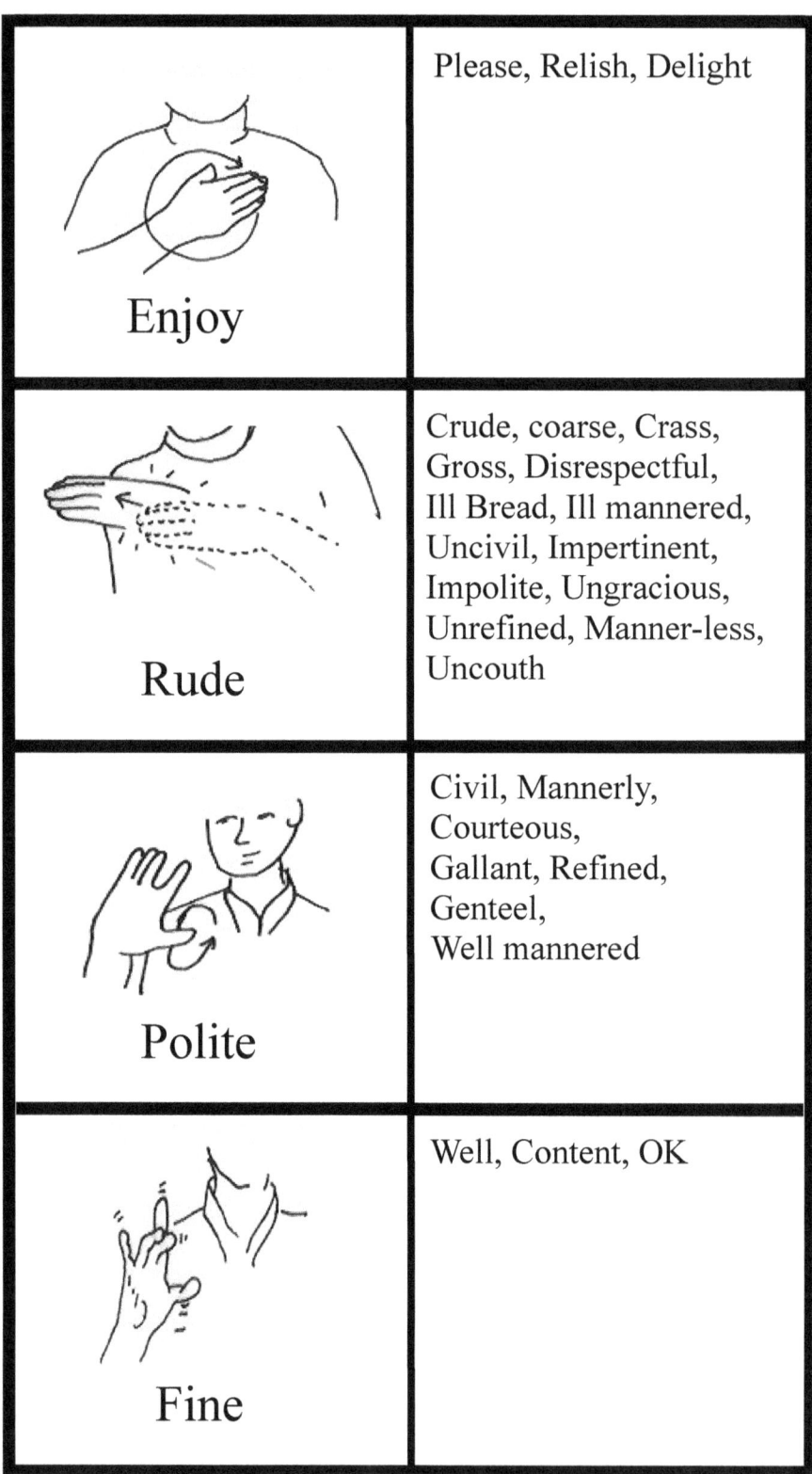

	Please, Relish, Delight
Enjoy	
Rude	Crude, coarse, Crass, Gross, Disrespectful, Ill Bread, Ill mannered, Uncivil, Impertinent, Impolite, Ungracious, Unrefined, Manner-less, Uncouth
Polite	Civil, Mannerly, Courteous, Gallant, Refined, Genteel, Well mannered
Fine	Well, Content, OK

Receive	Acceptance, Reception, Admission, Absorb, Acquire
Russia	Russian
Vacation	Retire, Take off, Holiday, Time off, Leave
Brave	Valiant, Valor, Bold, Undaunted, Gallant, Heroic, Audacity, Rash, Chivalry, Manliness, Grit, Mettle, Courageous, Guts, Spunk Spirit, Fearless, Intrepid, Un-fearful, Unafraid,

Performance	Act, Play, Perform, Opera
Complain	Gripe, Lament, Fuss, Murmur, Repine, Wail, Whine
Captain	Head, Chief, Commander, Counselor, Boss
Pittsburgh	Steel City

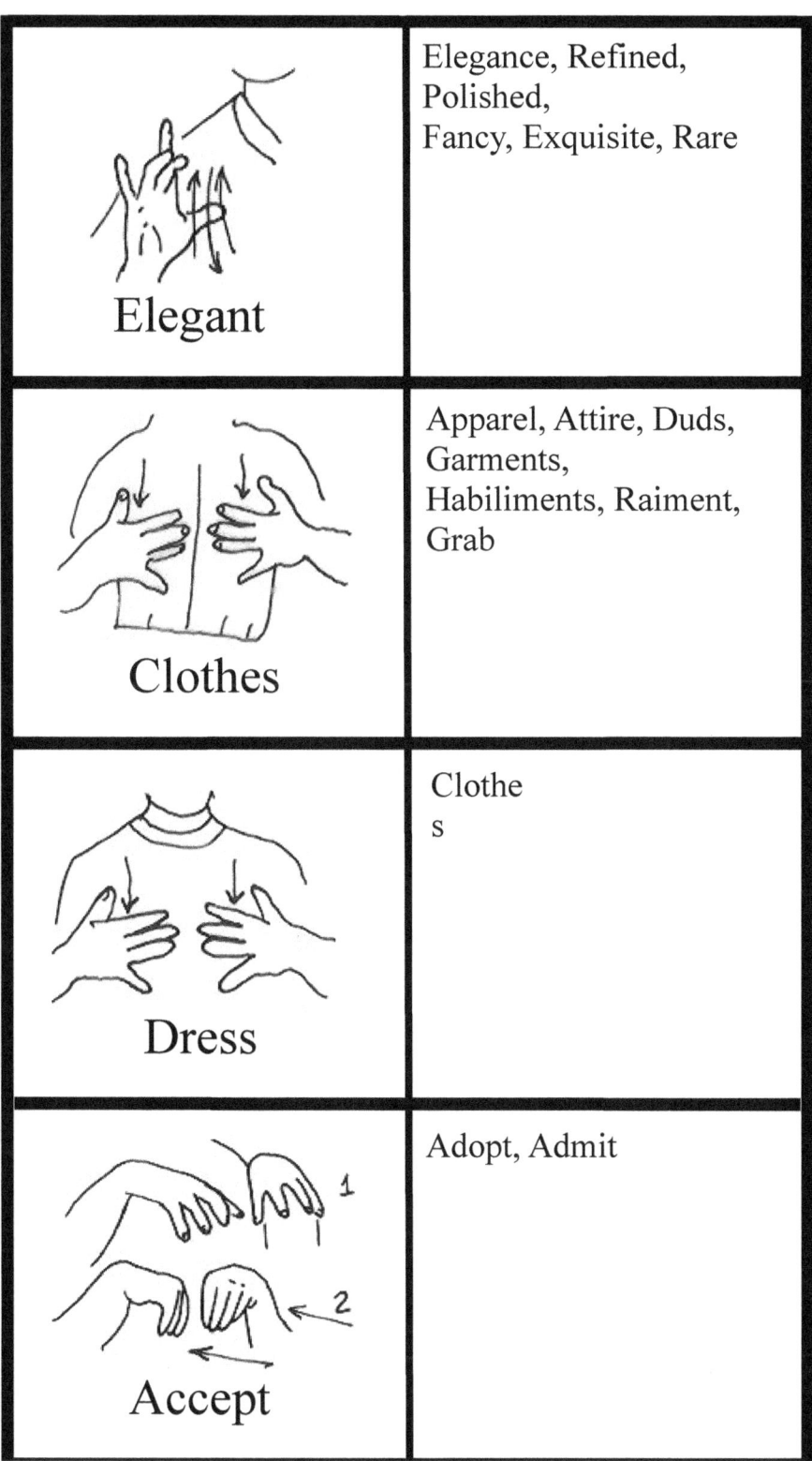

Elegant	Elegance, Refined, Polished, Fancy, Exquisite, Rare
Clothes	Apparel, Attire, Duds, Garments, Habiliments, Raiment, Grab
Dress	Clothes
Accept	Adopt, Admit

	Enlist, Available, Willing
Volunteer	
Alone	By yourself, Single, Separate, Only, Apart, Detached, Isolated, Removed, Unaccompanied, Solitary, Lone, Sole, Singular, Solo
We	Us
Since	From that time, Ago, Subsequently, In as much as, Because

Kingdom	Domain
Lord	Master, Ruler, Noble
Lazy	Passive, Indolent, Slothful, Idle, Laze, Loaf, Lunge, Vegetate, Bum
Personality	Character, Individuality, Deposition, Makeup, Nature, Temperament

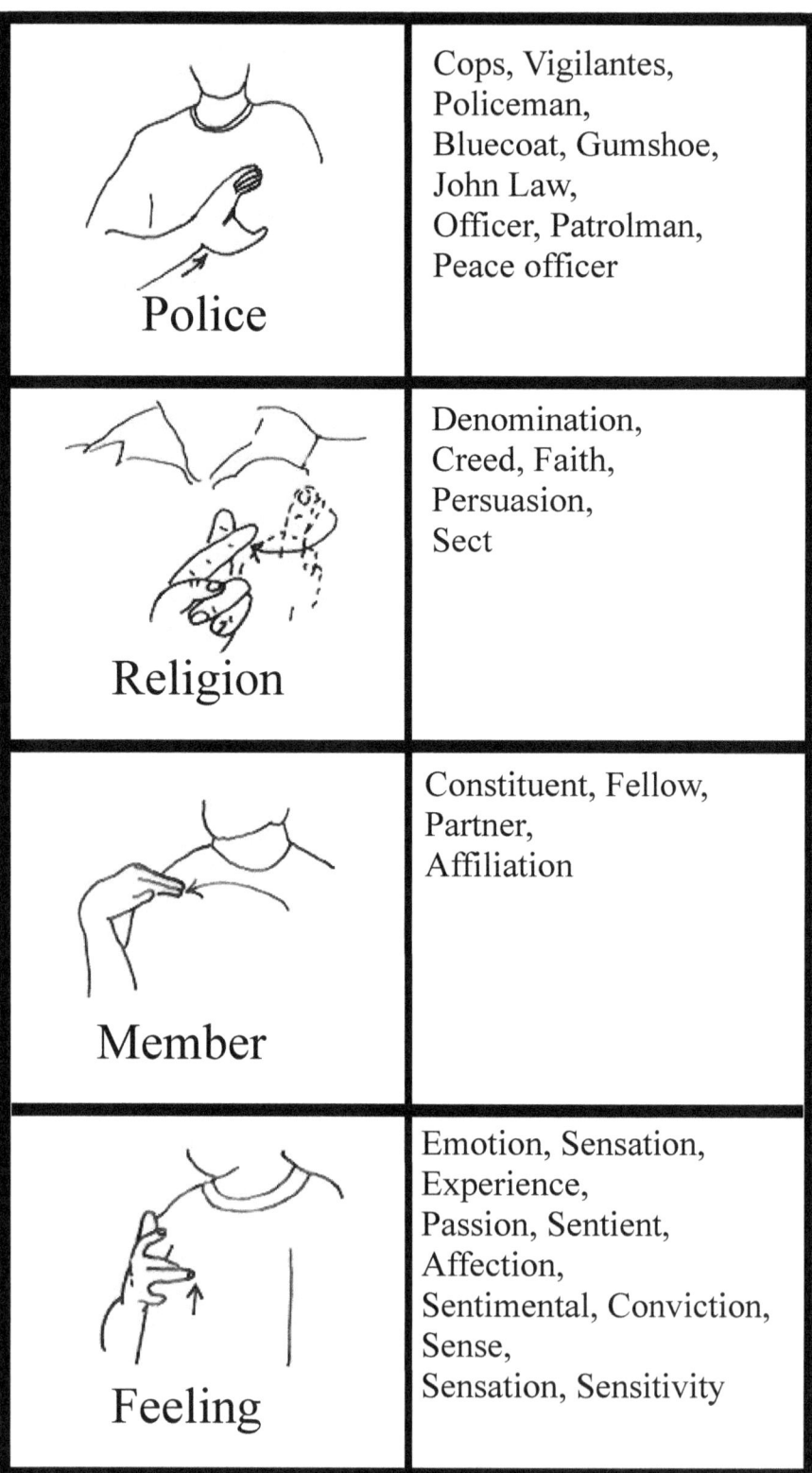

	Cops, Vigilantes, Policeman, Bluecoat, Gumshoe, John Law, Officer, Patrolman, Peace officer
Police	
	Denomination, Creed, Faith, Persuasion, Sect
Religion	
	Constituent, Fellow, Partner, Affiliation
Member	
	Emotion, Sensation, Experience, Passion, Sentient, Affection, Sentimental, Conviction, Sense, Sensation, Sensitivity
Feeling	

Heart	Center, Care, Core, Root
King	Head of, Ruler, Monarch, Royalty, Emperor, Sovereign, Magnate, Baron, Mogul, Czar
Queen	Ruler, Monarch, Royalty, Sovereign
Prince	Princess, Magnate, Baron, Baroness

Sensitive	Perceptive, Tender, Susceptible, Sentimental, Perspective, Impressionable, Precarious, Touchy
Excite	Vibrant, Uncontrollable, Thrill, Quicken, Frenzy, Elated, Exhilarated, Stimulated, Roused, Innervated
Young	Youthful, Juvenile, Immature, Child, Minor, Adolescent, Callow, Green, Unfledged, Unripe, Youthful
Live	Reside, Address, Abide, Exist, Bide, Dwell, Subsist

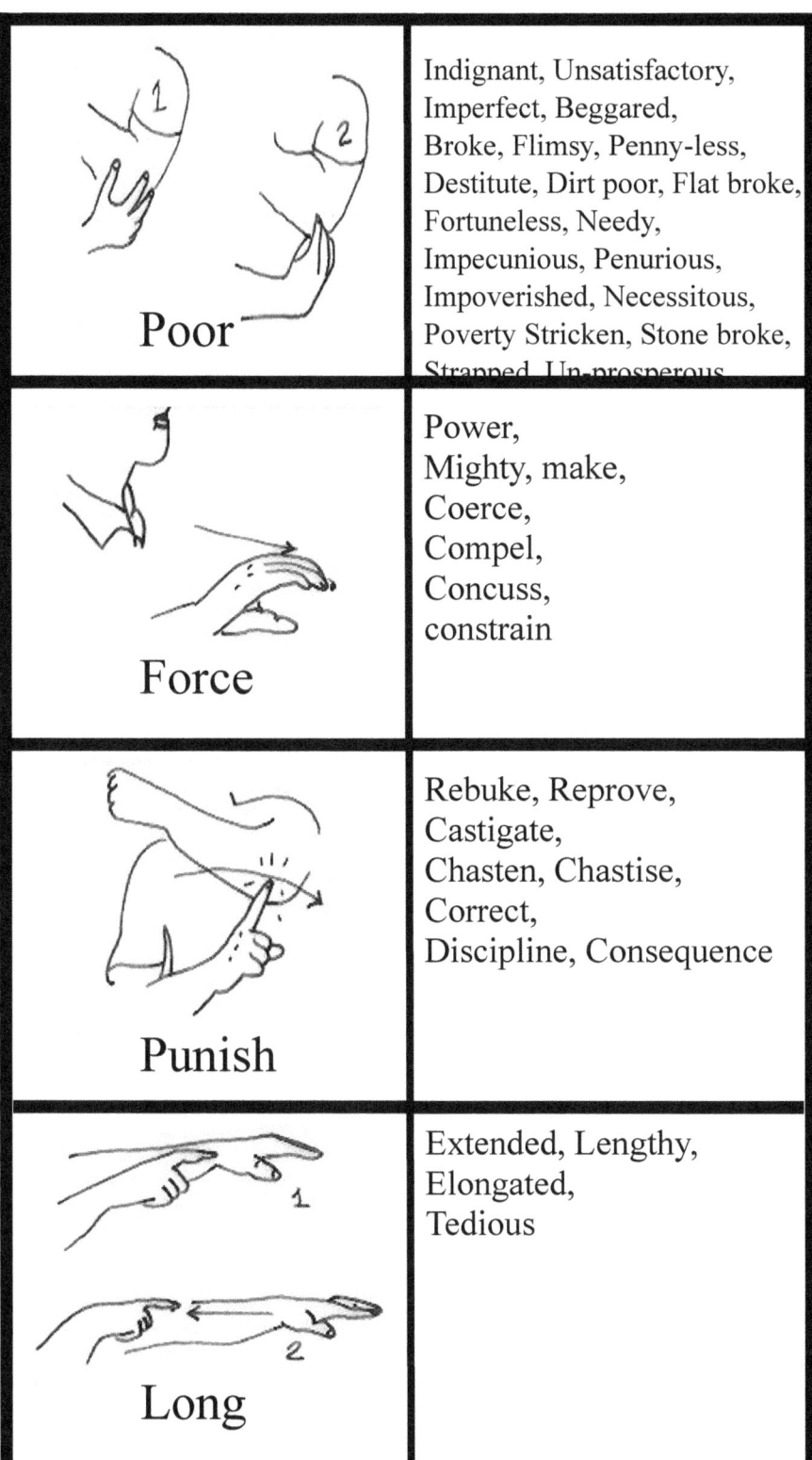

Poor	Indignant, Unsatisfactory, Imperfect, Beggared, Broke, Flimsy, Penny-less, Destitute, Dirt poor, Flat broke, Fortuneless, Needy, Impecunious, Penurious, Impoverished, Necessitous, Poverty Stricken, Stone broke, Strapped, Un-prosperous
Force	Power, Mighty, make, Coerce, Compel, Concuss, constrain
Punish	Rebuke, Reprove, Castigate, Chasten, Chastise, Correct, Discipline, Consequence
Long	Extended, Lengthy, Elongated, Tedious

	Lamb, Ewe, Kid
Sheep	
Steal	Take, Apprehend, Thievery, Rob, Theft, Larceny, Loot, Lift, Pinch, Purloining, Abduct, Burglarize, Snatch
Bridge	Crossover, Span, Viaduct, Undercross
Temptation	Coercion, Persuasion, Enticement, Snare, Allure, -ment, Bait, Lure, Come on, Decoy, Inveiglement, Seducement, Siren Song, Snare

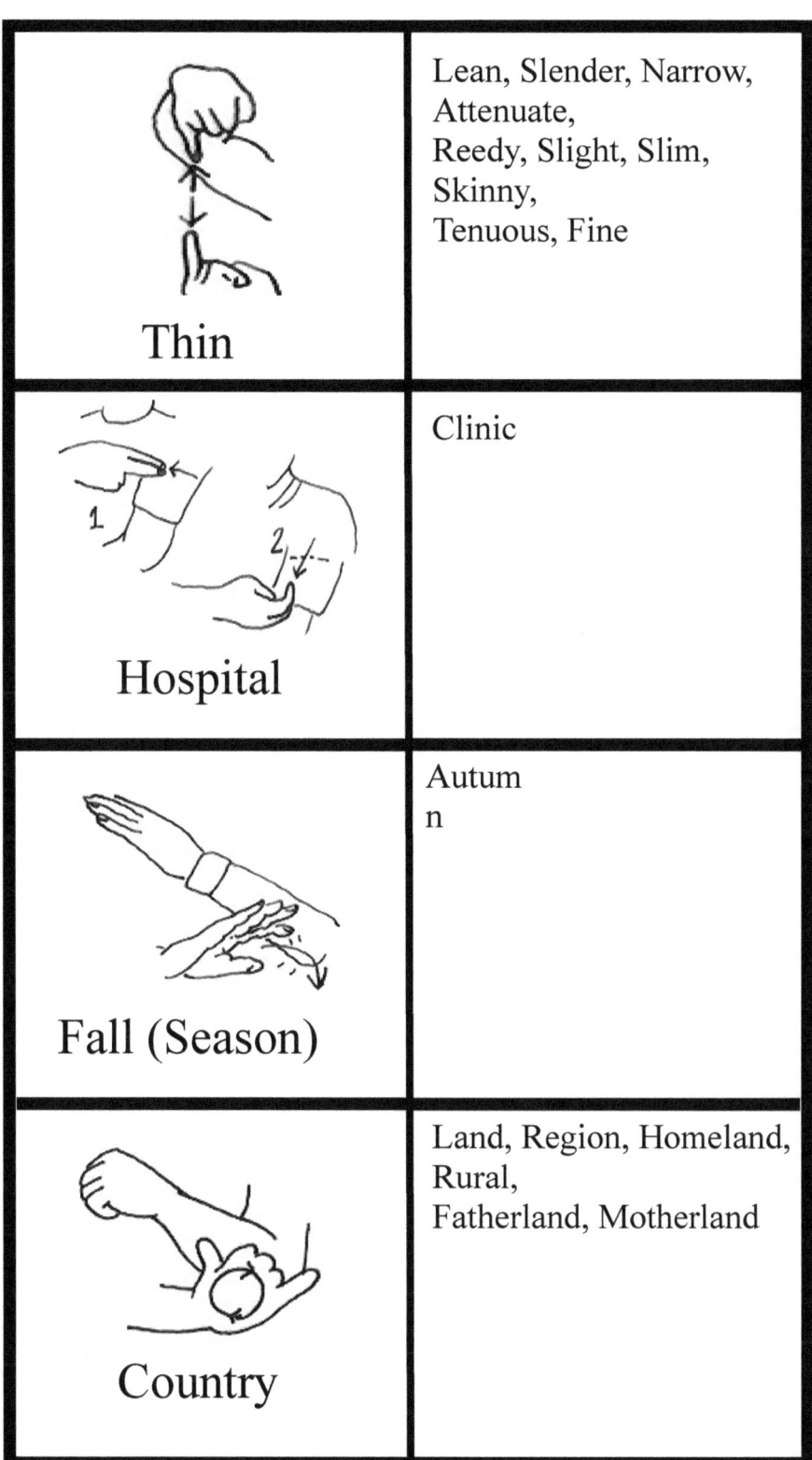

	Lean, Slender, Narrow, Attenuate, Reedy, Slight, Slim, Skinny, Tenuous, Fine
Thin	
	Clinic
Hospital	
	Autumn
Fall (Season)	
	Land, Region, Homeland, Rural, Fatherland, Motherland
Country	

Lock	Secure, Fasten, Close
Defeat	Beat, Overpower, Rout, Blast, Crush, Dust, Lick, Curry, Thrash, Drub, Prevail, Lambaste, Mop up, Triumph, Skunk, Whip, Overrun, Overcome, Upend, Overwhelm, Shellac, Trounce, Smother, Steam roll, Wallop, Whomp, Control
Establish	Found, Start, Root, Build, Foundation, Confirm, Secure, Set up, Install Institute, Create, Constitute, Organize
Improve	Advance, Ascent, Build up, Develop, Enhance, Promotion, Progress, Perk up, Make better, Ameliorate, Convalesce, Grain, Look up, Mend, Recuperate

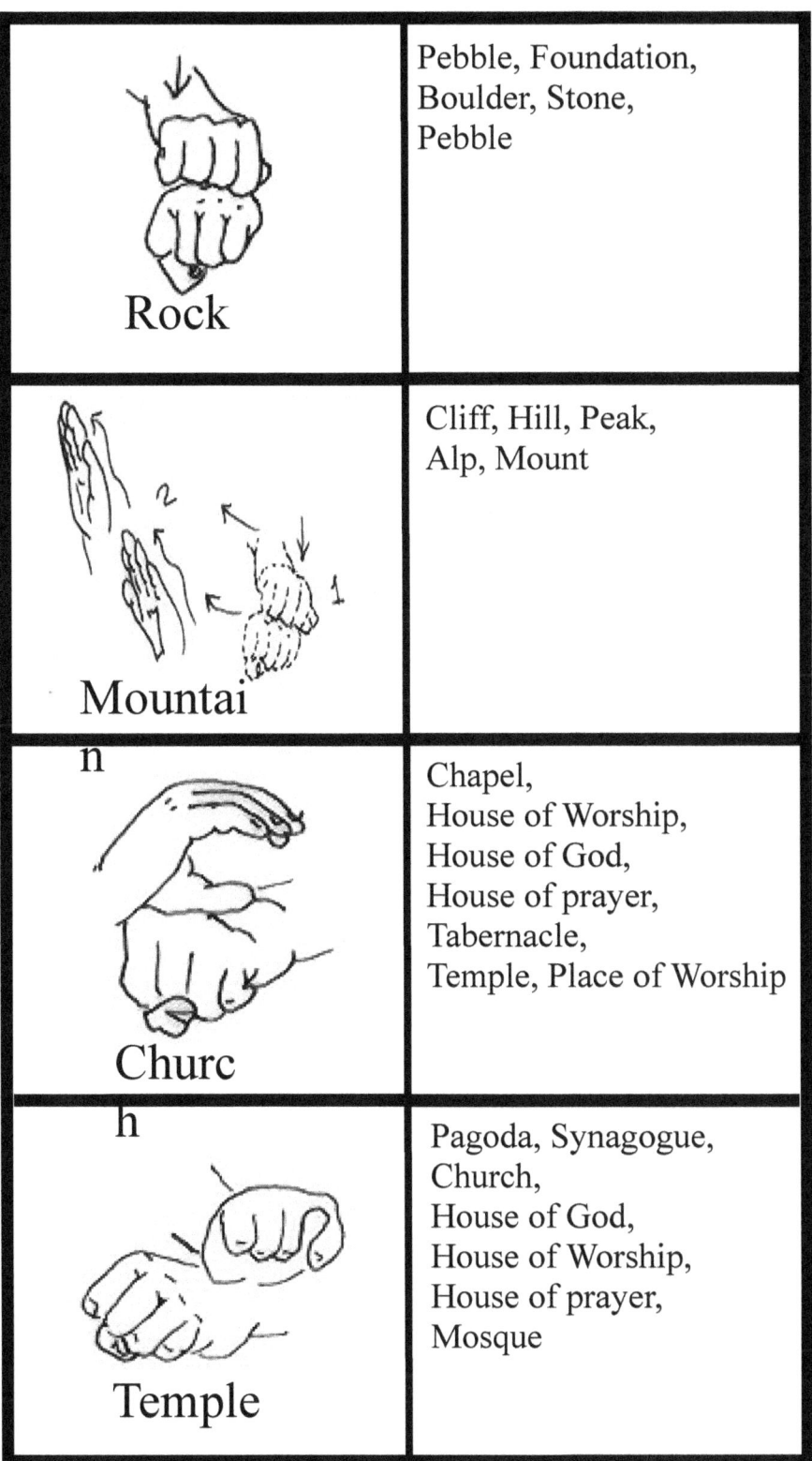

Rock	Pebble, Foundation, Boulder, Stone, Pebble
Mountain	Cliff, Hill, Peak, Alp, Mount
Church	Chapel, House of Worship, House of God, House of prayer, Tabernacle, Temple, Place of Worship
Temple	Pagoda, Synagogue, Church, House of God, House of Worship, House of prayer, Mosque

Work	Drudgery, Grind, Labor, Toil, Job, Trade, Employment, Occupation, Pursuit, Operate, Function
Busy	Active, Business, Firm, Hard work, Industry, -ing, Livelihood, In use, Engrossed, Concern, Occupied, Establishment, Bustling, Function, Hustling, Duty, Province, Role, Industry, Hopping,
Fin	Acquisition, Come across, Discover, Detect, -ing, -ound, Locate, Espial, Strike, Spot, Encounter, Hit on
Engaged	Betrothed, Espoused, Intended, Affianced

Deteriorate	Decline, Lessen, Degenerate, Dis-improve, Disintegrate, Retrograde, Sink, Worsen, Digress
Slow	Creep, Crawl, Leisurely, Dilatory, Retardation, Stroll, Plod, Trudge, Laggard, Un-hasty, Unhurried
Sing	Carol, Chant, Harmony, Melody, Melodic, Music, Song
Blame	Accuse, Fault, Cause, Condemn, -ation, Criticism, Culpability, Denunciation, Onus, Rap, reprove, Reprehensible

Time	Duration, Period, Span, Space, Spell
Dut y	Commitment, Commission, Charge, Liability, Onus, Obligation, Task, Responsibility, Assignment Devoir
Nurs e	Medical Attendant, R.N., L.V.N
Doctor	Chiropractor, Consultant, Physician, Surgeon, M.D., Holder of Doctoral degree, General Practitioner, Medico

	Spud, Tater
Potato	
Whiskey	Liquor, Moonshine, Booze, Hooch, Alcoholic beverage
Naked	Empty, Nothing on, Nude, Unclad, Honed, Undressed, Keen, Au natural, Bluff, Acute, Raw, Stripped, Wetted, Acute, Birthday suit, Sharp, Vacant
Bal	Bare headed, Baldly, Hairless, Glabrous, Smooth headed, Naked head, Vacant

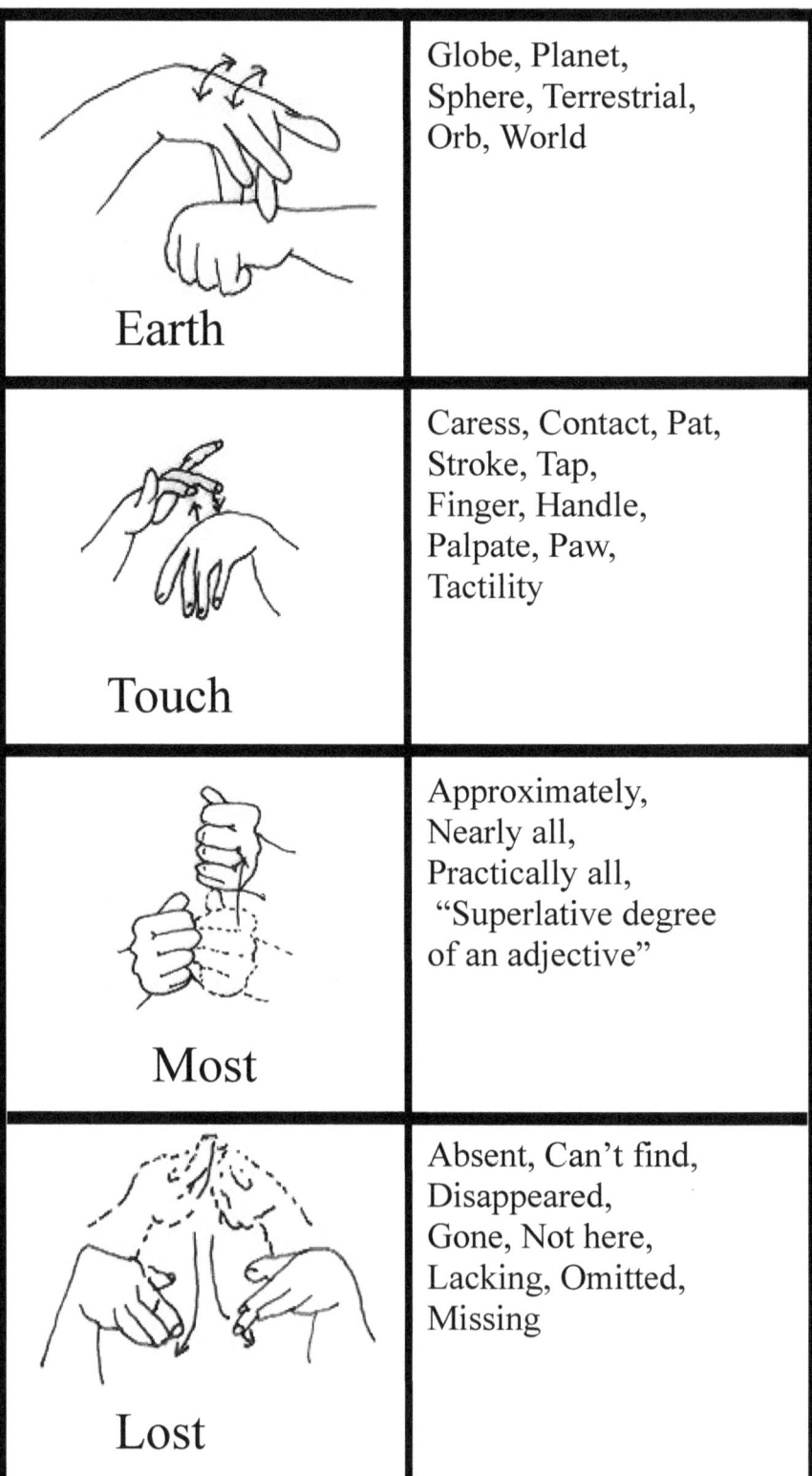

Earth	Globe, Planet, Sphere, Terrestrial, Orb, World
Touch	Caress, Contact, Pat, Stroke, Tap, Finger, Handle, Palpate, Paw, Tactility
Most	Approximately, Nearly all, Practically all, "Superlative degree of an adjective"
Lost	Absent, Can't find, Disappeared, Gone, Not here, Lacking, Omitted, Missing

Div	Leap, Plunge, Jump, Lunge
Island	Isle
Institution	Asylum, Company, Residential School, Institute, Organization
Advice	Affect, Counsel, Guidance, Suggestion, Recommendation, Influence

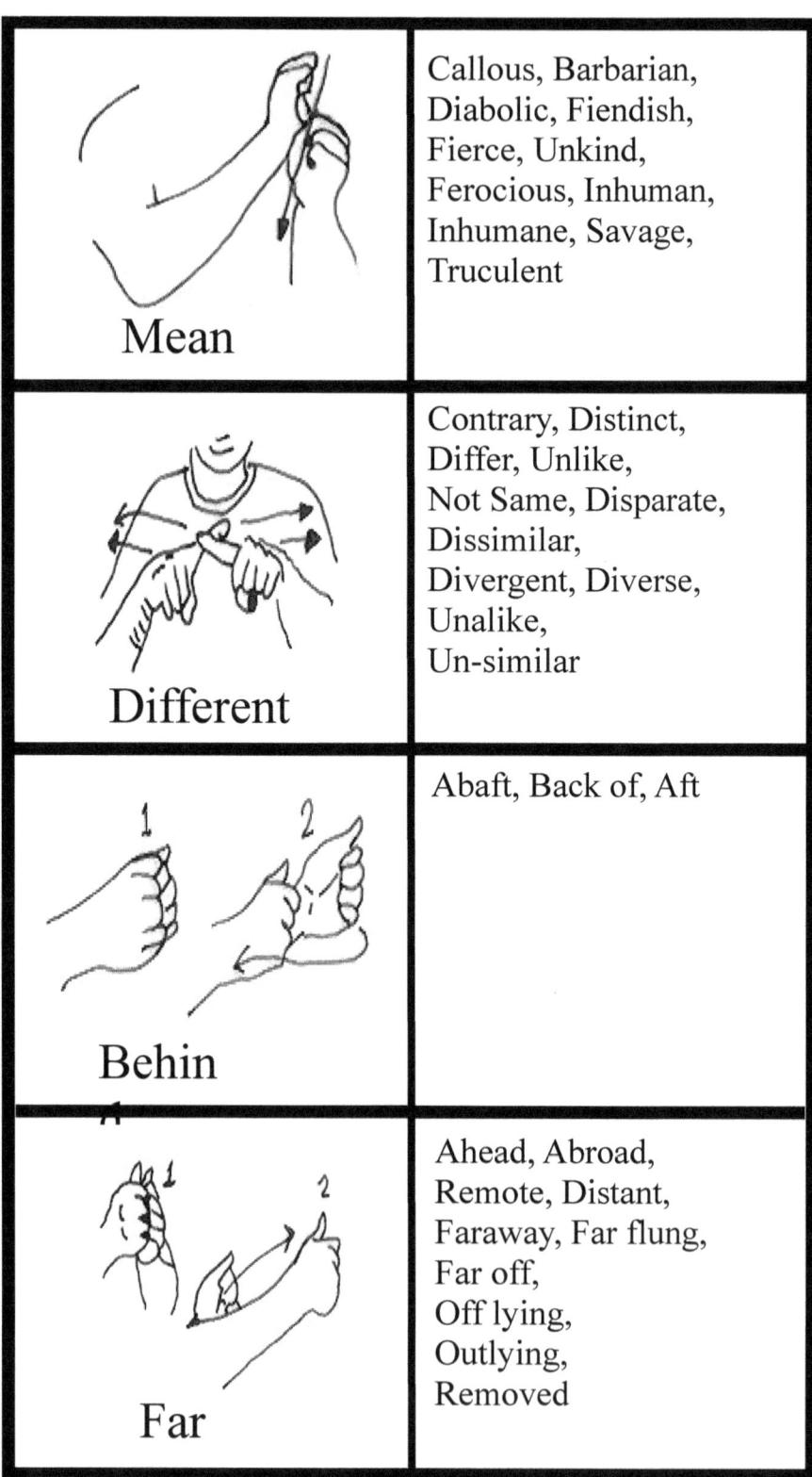

Mean	Callous, Barbarian, Diabolic, Fiendish, Fierce, Unkind, Ferocious, Inhuman, Inhumane, Savage, Truculent
Different	Contrary, Distinct, Differ, Unlike, Not Same, Disparate, Dissimilar, Divergent, Diverse, Unalike, Un-similar
Behin	Abaft, Back of, Aft
Far	Ahead, Abroad, Remote, Distant, Faraway, Far flung, Far off, Off lying, Outlying, Removed

	Each one, Every one
Ever	
Chas	Trail, Ensue, Follow, Chivy, Pursue
Catch	Caught up, Not behind
Hel	Aid, Assist, -ant, Helper, Lend a hand

Support	Advocate, In favor of, Supporting, Back, Side with, Bolster, Sustain
Assistant	Aid, Aide, Attendant, Helper
Full	Chock-full, Packed, Brimful, Awash, Brimming, Cram-full, Crammed, Jammed, Replete, Stuffed, Fed up, Laden, Voluminous
Enough	Adequate, Plenty, Sufficient

	Joe, Caf, Java
Coffee	
	Clean, Cleanse, Lave, Scrub
Wash	
	Yearly, Once a year, Annual
Year	
	Backslidden, Fall behind, Lapse, Recidivate, Relapse
Backslide	

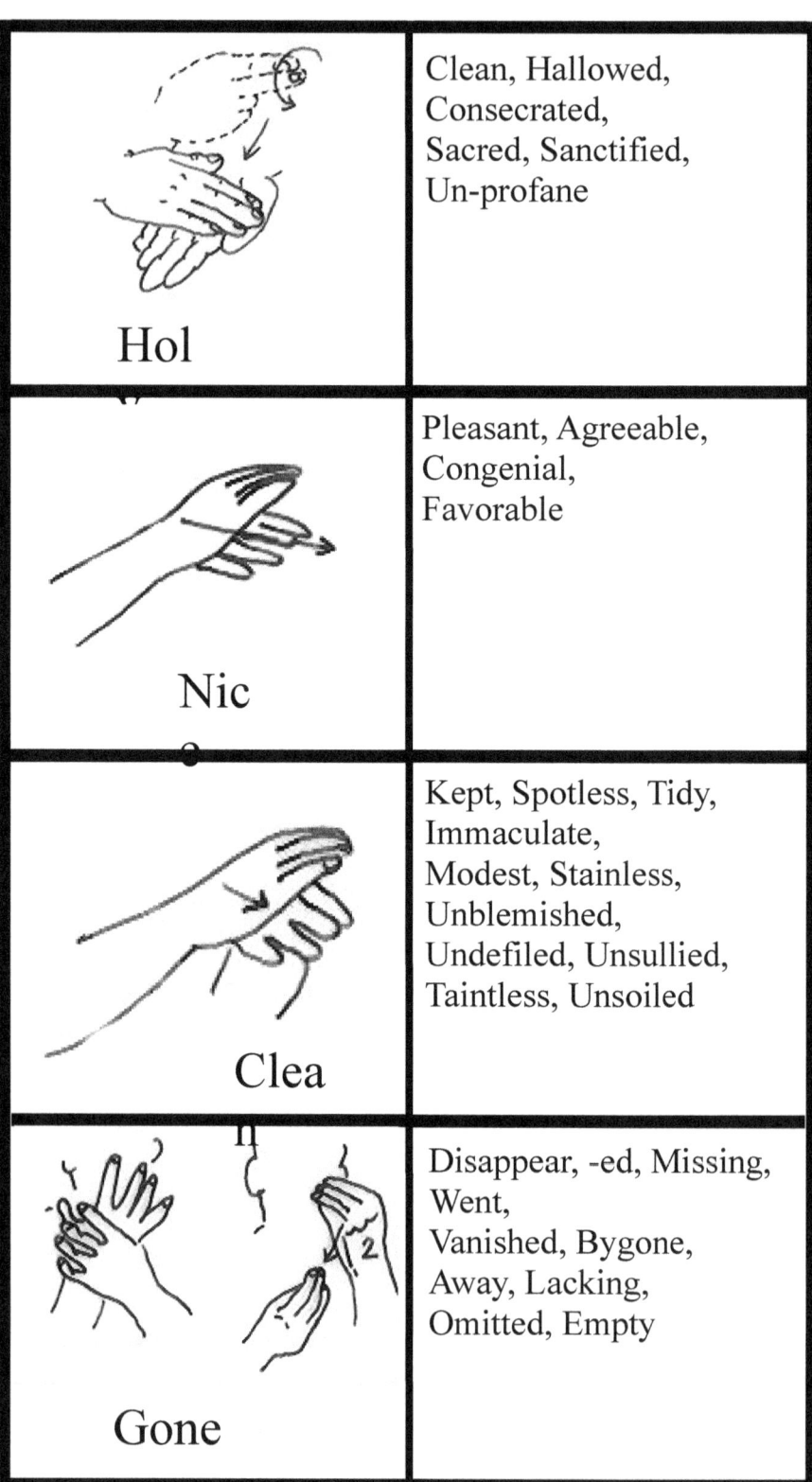

| | Clean, Hallowed, Consecrated, Sacred, Sanctified, Un-profane |

Hol

| | Pleasant, Agreeable, Congenial, Favorable |

Nic

| | Kept, Spotless, Tidy, Immaculate, Modest, Stainless, Unblemished, Undefiled, Unsullied, Taintless, Unsoiled |

Clea

| | Disappear, -ed, Missing, Went, Vanished, Bygone, Away, Lacking, Omitted, Empty |

Gone

Operation	Surgery, Incision, Scar
Remove	Deduct, Eliminate, Get rid of, Subtract, Liquidate
Iron	Ferric, Ferrous, Metal, Metallic, Oxide
Practice	Drill, Repeat, Rehearsal

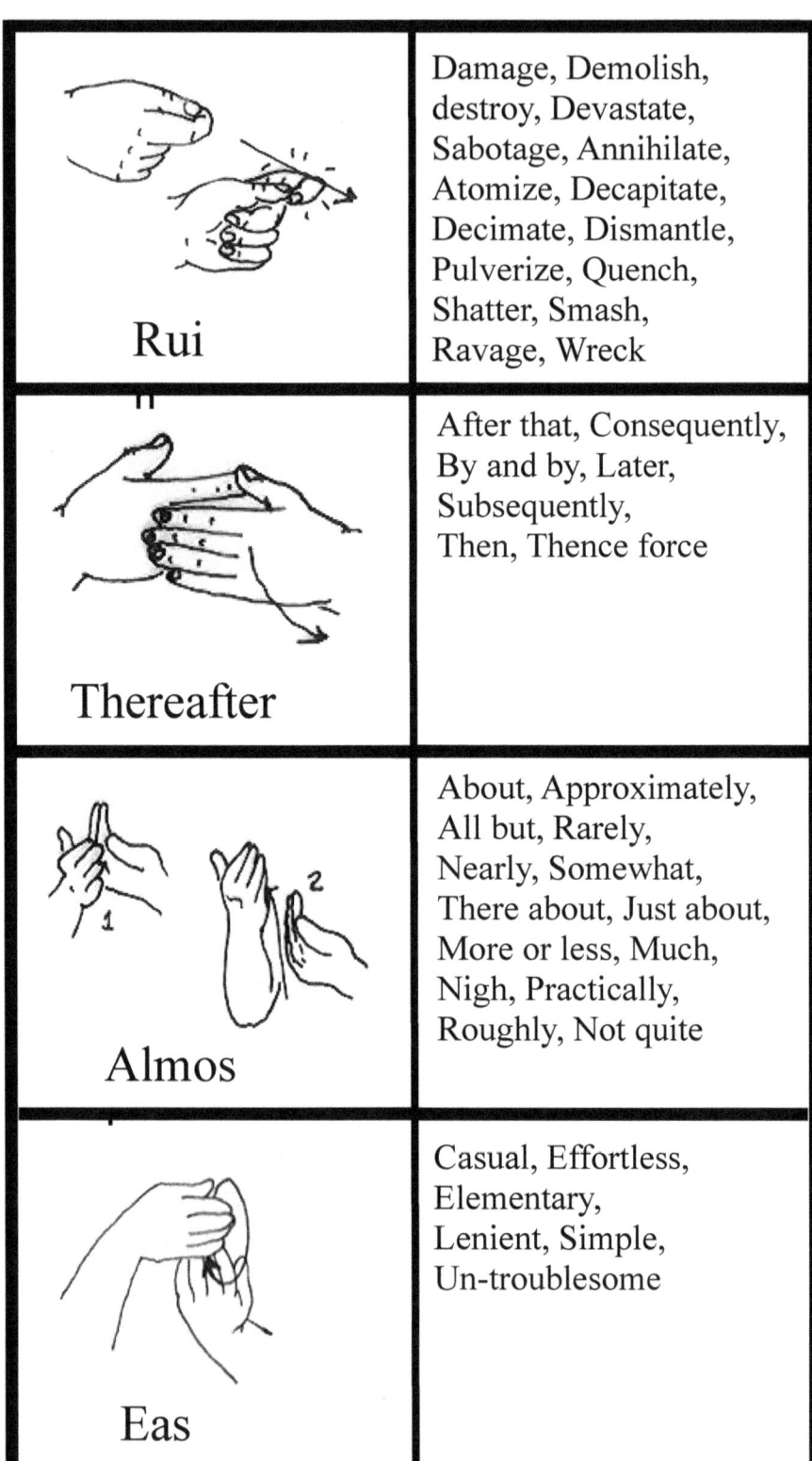

Rui	Damage, Demolish, destroy, Devastate, Sabotage, Annihilate, Atomize, Decapitate, Decimate, Dismantle, Pulverize, Quench, Shatter, Smash, Ravage, Wreck
Thereafter	After that, Consequently, By and by, Later, Subsequently, Then, Thence force
Almos	About, Approximately, All but, Rarely, Nearly, Somewhat, There about, Just about, More or less, Much, Nigh, Practically, Roughly, Not quite
Eas	Casual, Effortless, Elementary, Lenient, Simple, Un-troublesome

	Foremost, Headmost, Inaugural, Initial, Leading, Original, Primary, Prime
Firs	
	Ghost, Apparition, Bogey, Phantasm, Phantom, Revenant, Specter, Umbra, Wraith
Spirit	
	Comforter, Holy Ghost
Holy Spirit	
	Coddle, Pamper, Cater to, Cosset, Cotton, Humor, Indulge
Spoil-pet too much	

Day	Today
Morning	Daybreak, Daylight, Dawn, Before noon, Forenoon, Sunup, Sunrise, Morn, Aurora
Night	Evening, Last night, Sunset, Tonight, Twilight, Nighttime, Night tide, Nocturnal
Midnight	12 P.M. Witching hour

	Snack
Sandwich	
Forgive	Absolve, Excuse, Exempt, Pardon, Waive, Condone, Remit
Excus~~e~~	Exempt, Forgive, Pardon, Waive, Condon, Remit, Alibi, Plea, Pretext
Fired	Canned, Discharged, Dismissed, Let go, Sent packing, Terminated, Axed, Booted out, Sacked

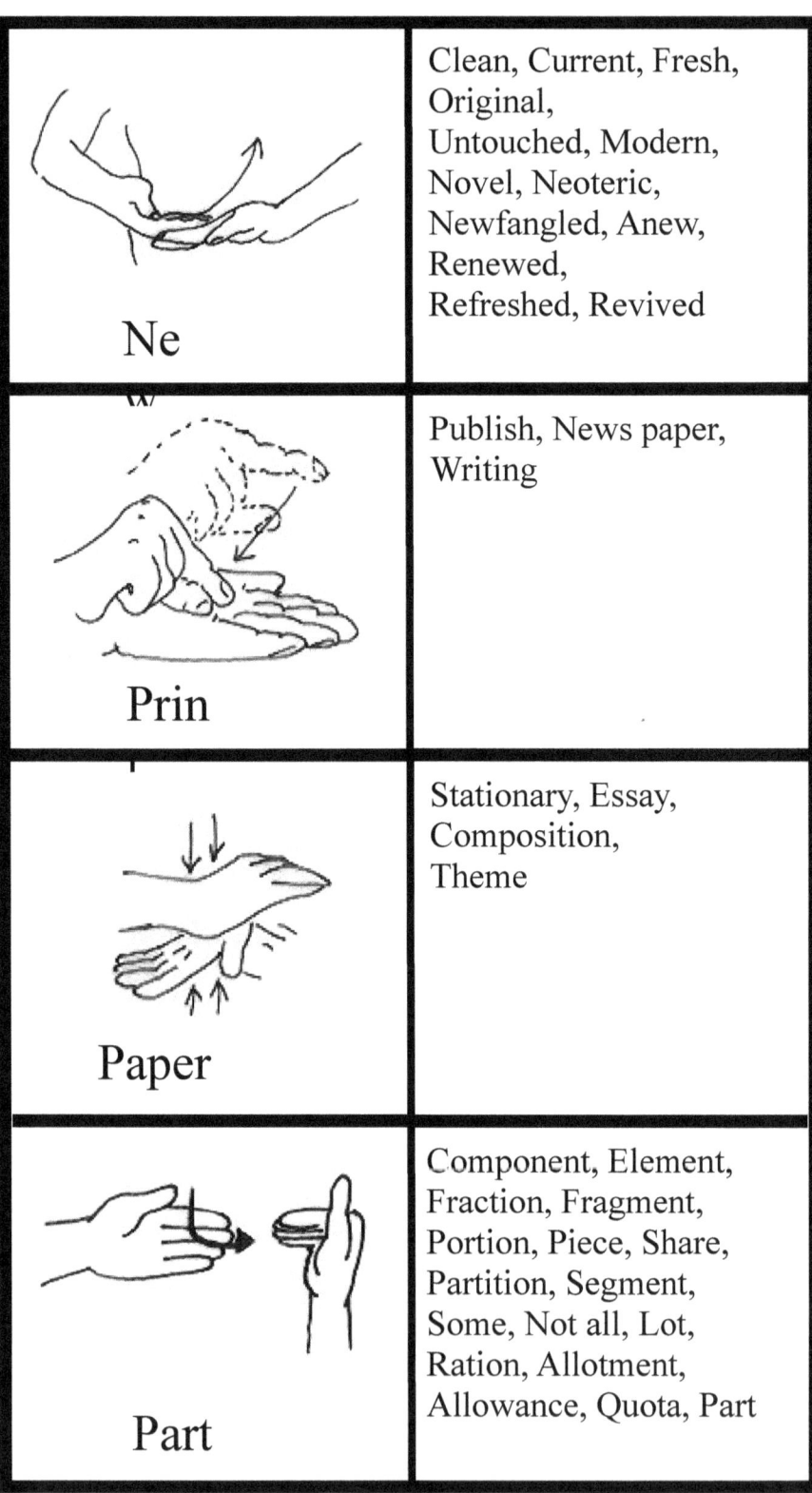

New	Clean, Current, Fresh, Original, Untouched, Modern, Novel, Neoteric, Newfangled, Anew, Renewed, Refreshed, Revived
Print	Publish, News paper, Writing
Paper	Stationary, Essay, Composition, Theme
Part	Component, Element, Fraction, Fragment, Portion, Piece, Share, Partition, Segment, Some, Not all, Lot, Ration, Allotment, Allowance, Quota, Part

	High noon, Midday, Noontime
Noon	
Slic	Cut, Piece, Portion, Thin piece, Section, Sharing, Wedge, Carve, Cleave, Dissect, Disserve
Brea	Loaf
Cheap	Bargain, Economical, Low cost, Low price, Inexpensive, Reasonable, Un-costly, Cheesy, Paltry, Shabby, Scummy, Shoddy, Sleazy, Trashy, Trumpery

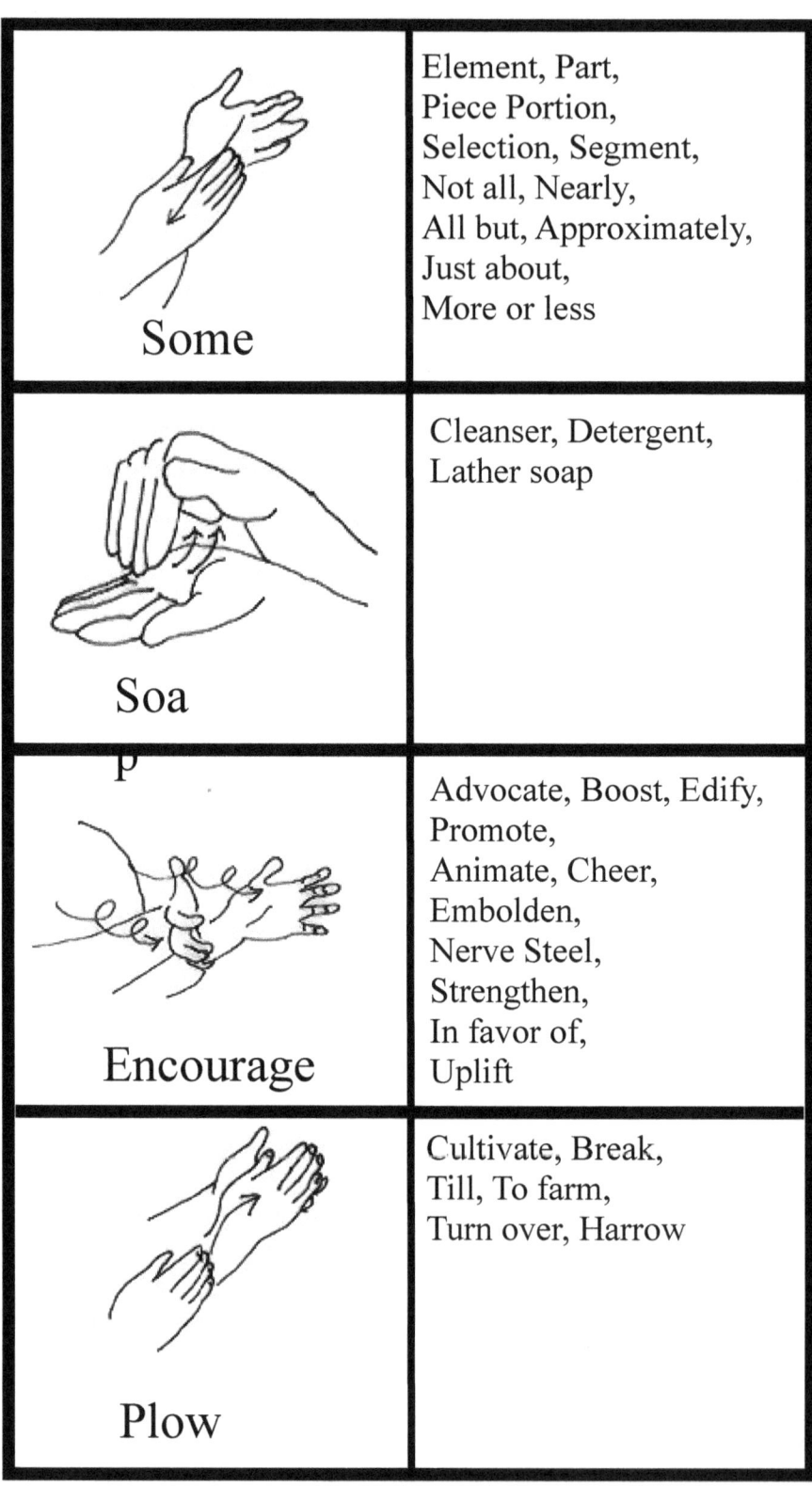

Some	Element, Part, Piece Portion, Selection, Segment, Not all, Nearly, All but, Approximately, Just about, More or less
Soap	Cleanser, Detergent, Lather soap
Encourage	Advocate, Boost, Edify, Promote, Animate, Cheer, Embolden, Nerve Steel, Strengthen, In favor of, Uplift
Plow	Cultivate, Break, Till, To farm, Turn over, Harrow

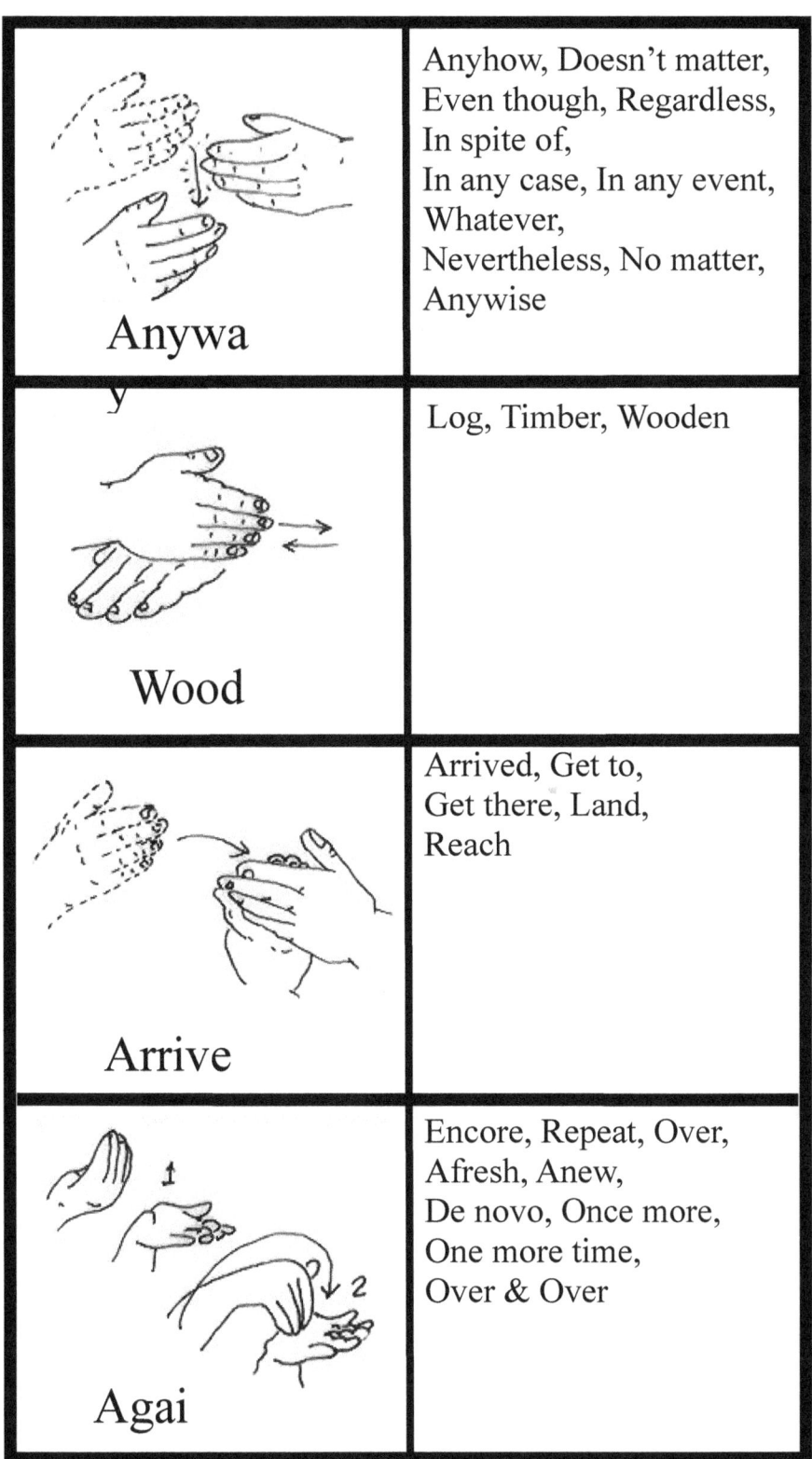

Anywa y	Anyhow, Doesn't matter, Even though, Regardless, In spite of, In any case, In any event, Whatever, Nevertheless, No matter, Anywise
Wood	Log, Timber, Wooden
Arrive	Arrived, Get to, Get there, Land, Reach
Agai	Encore, Repeat, Over, Afresh, Anew, De novo, Once more, One more time, Over & Over

Often	Again and again, Constantly, Oftentimes, Regularly, Frequently, Much many times, More than once, Oft, Recurrently, Repeatedly, Over and over, Time and again
Tree	Forest, Trees, Timber, Woods, Woodland
Flag	Banner, Banderole, Bannerol, Burgee, Ensign, Pendant, Pennant, Standard, Streamer
Chees e	Curds

	Cross, Thwart, Beyond, crosswise, Crossways, Cross over, Transversely, Over
Across	
	Every, Entirely, Total, -ly, Inclusive, Whole, All in all, Altogether, In toto, Complete, Include
All	
	Allowed, Fine, Permitted, OK
All right	
	Pronto, Rapid, Right away, Speedily, Full tilt, Suddenly, Swift, Immediately, Promptly Fleet Breakneck, Expeditious, Hastily, Post Haste, Snappy, Chop chop, Presto,
Fast	

Close	Shut, Slam
Gat e	Hinge, Fence opening
Nea r	Almost, Approach, Close by, Close to, Neighborhood, Next to, Near at hand, Nearby, Nigh Toward
Retaliat e	Avenge, Get even, Revenge, Reciprocate, recompense, Requite, Vindicate

	Internal, Inner, Inside
In	
Out	Outside, Leave, Get out, Go out
Resign	Back out, Drop out, Quit, Withdraw, Step down, relinquish, Abandon, Cede, Yield, Demit, Abdicate, Renounce
Lesso	Course, Chapter, Section, Exercise

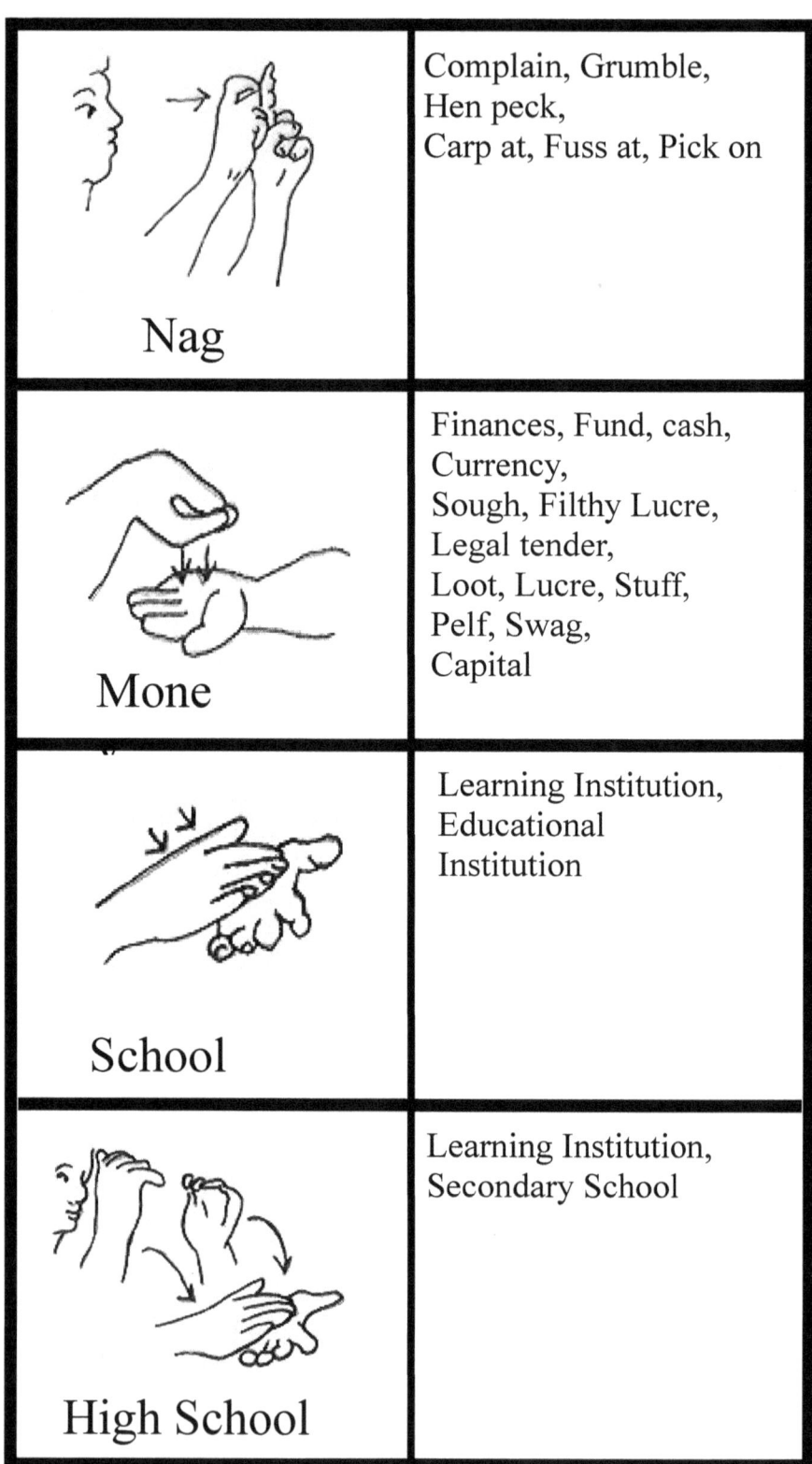

Nag	Complain, Grumble, Hen peck, Carp at, Fuss at, Pick on
Mone	Finances, Fund, cash, Currency, Sough, Filthy Lucre, Legal tender, Loot, Lucre, Stuff, Pelf, Swag, Capital
School	Learning Institution, Educational Institution
High School	Learning Institution, Secondary School

Warm	Alert, Admonish, Reprove, Call out, Caution, Forewarn
Call	Summon, Call in
Invit	Hire, Invitation, Usher, Welcome, Bid
Weak	Feeble, Flimsy, Fragile, Frail, Insubstantial, Puny, Unsound, Weary, Wobbly, Fatigue

Lear	Acquire knowledge, Educate
Stud	Concentrate, Practice, Rehearse
Copy	Duplicate, Imitate, Mimic, Model, Reproduce, Carbon, Ditto, Facsimile, Republication, Replica, Replicate, Replication
Cancel	Annul, Call off, Drop plan, Delete, Condemn, Correct, Criticize, Cross out, Find fault

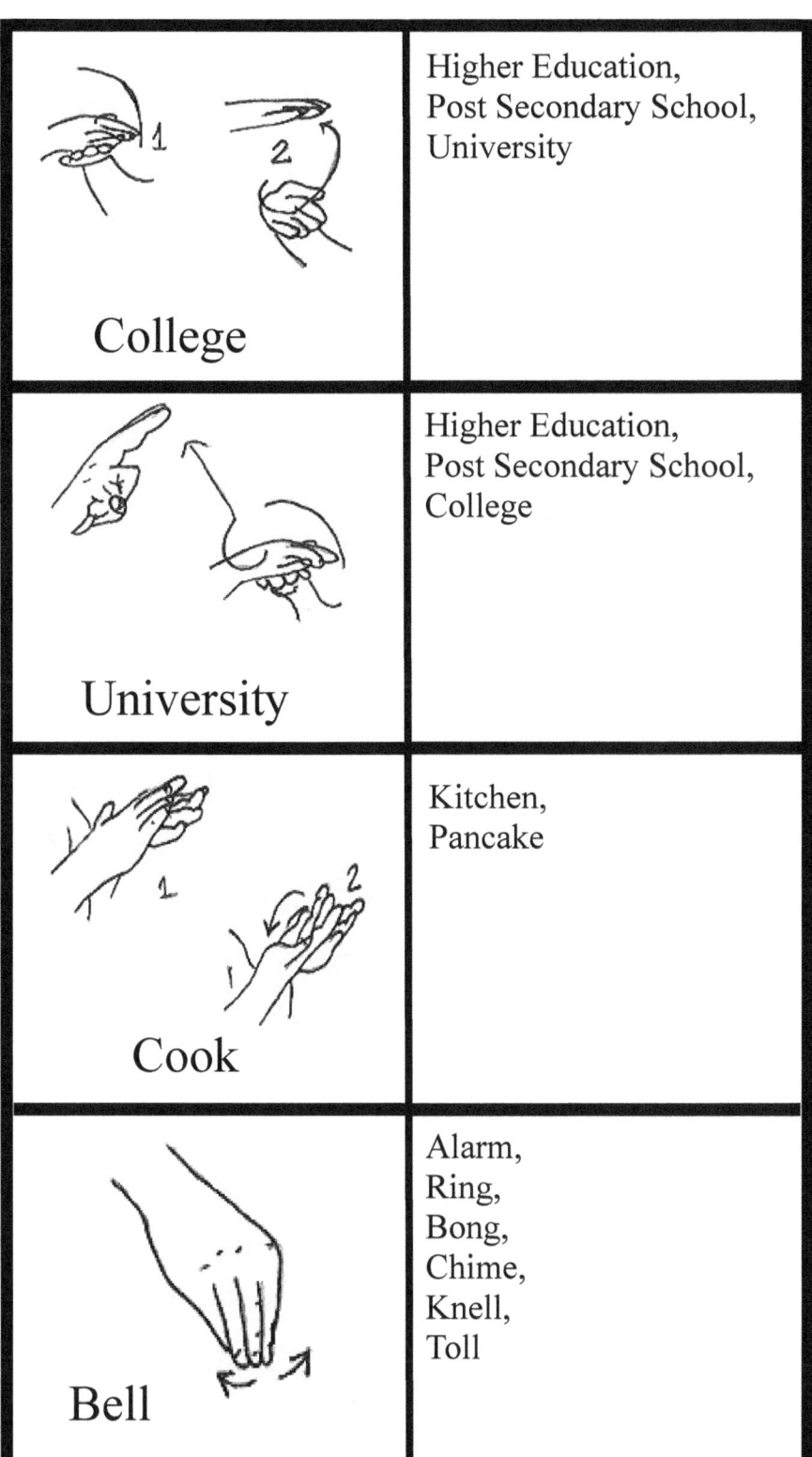

	Higher Education, Post Secondary School, University
College	
University	Higher Education, Post Secondary School, College
Cook	Kitchen, Pancake
Bell	Alarm, Ring, Bong, Chime, Knell, Toll

	Babble, Cook, Heat, Bristle, Flare up, Seethe, Churn, Ferment, Simmer, Smolder, Stew, Parboil
Boil	
Fire	Burn, Flame, Inferno, Blaze
Hell	Burn forever, Abyss, Blazes, Gahanna, Hades, Inferno, Netherworld, Pit, Sheol, Lake of fire
Glor	Glorious, Exult, Jubilate, Exalt, Glorify, Praise, Worship

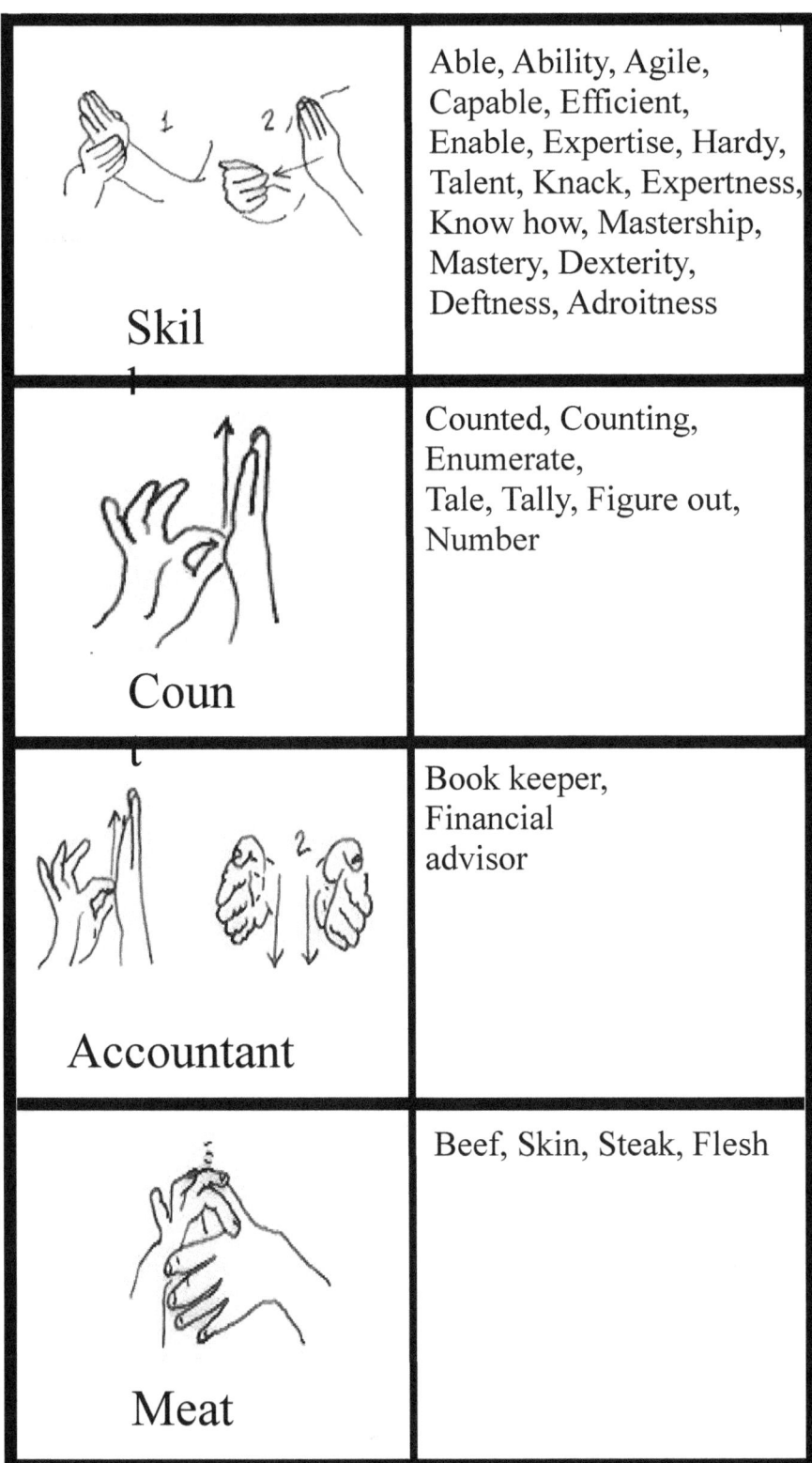

	Able, Ability, Agile, Capable, Efficient, Enable, Expertise, Hardy, Talent, Knack, Expertness, Know how, Mastership, Mastery, Dexterity, Deftness, Adroitness
Skill	
Count	Counted, Counting, Enumerate, Tale, Tally, Figure out, Number
Accountant	Book keeper, Financial advisor
Meat	Beef, Skin, Steak, Flesh

Boil	Babble, Cook, Heat, Bristle, Flare up, Seethe, Churn, Ferment, Simmer, Smolder, Stew, Parboil
Fire	Burn, Flame, Inferno, Blaze
Hell	Burn forever, Abyss, Blazes, Gahanna, Hades, Inferno, Netherworld, Pit, Sheol, Lake of fire
Glor	Glorious, Exult, Jubilate, Exalt, Glorify, Praise, Worship

126

	Able, Ability, Agile, Capable, Efficient, Enable, Expertise, Hardy, Talent, Knack, Expertness, Know how, Mastership, Mastery, Dexterity, Deftness, Adroitness
Skil	
	Counted, Counting, Enumerate, Tale, Tally, Figure out, Number
Coun	
	Book keeper, Financial advisor
Accountant	
	Beef, Skin, Steak, Flesh
Meat	

Tall	Big, High, Height, Altitudinous
Deep	Depth, Detail, Abysmal, Profound
Kill	Murder, Slay, Slaughter, Carry off, Finish, Take out, Snuff
What	What for?, What's up?, Huh?, Whatever

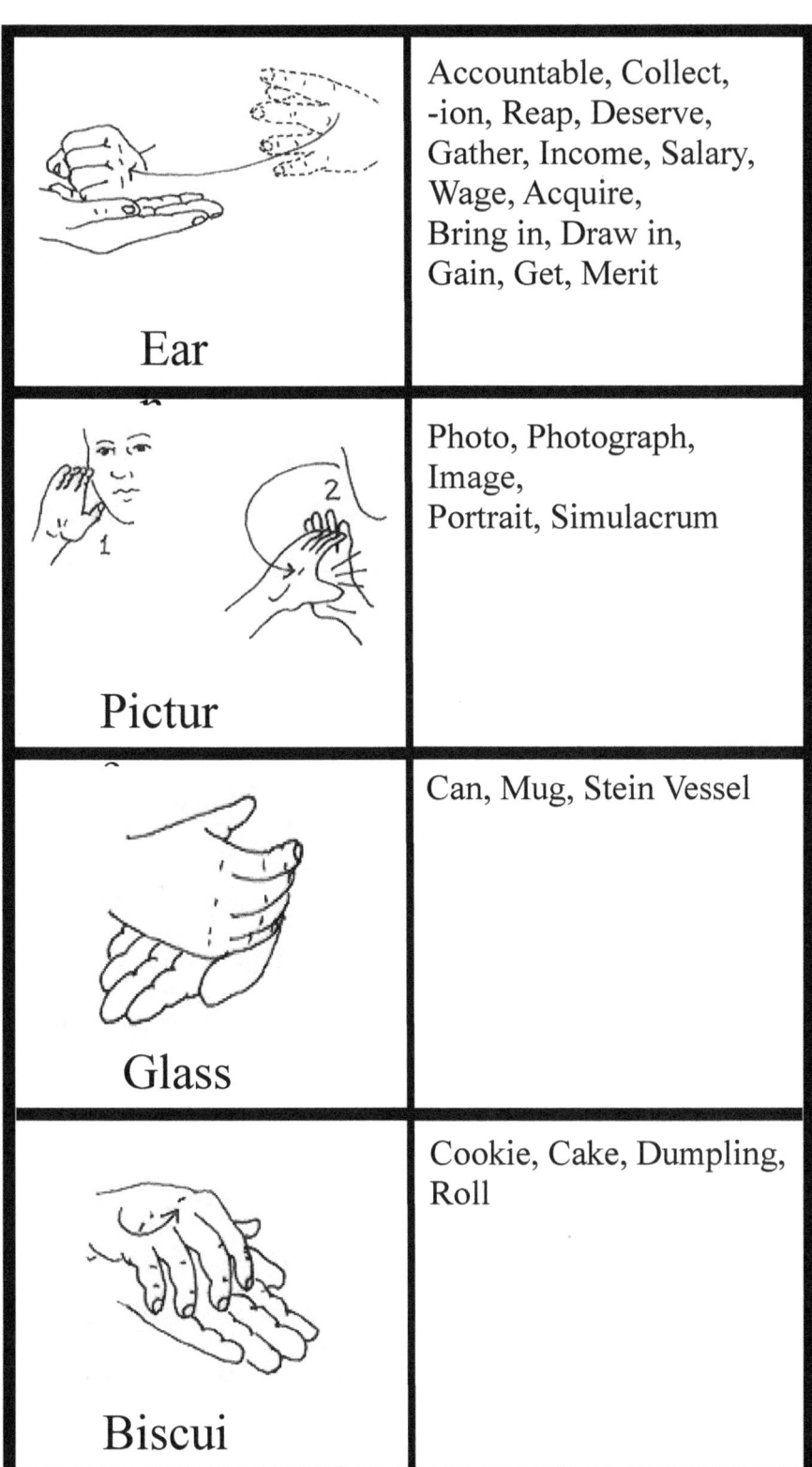

Ear	Accountable, Collect, -ion, Reap, Deserve, Gather, Income, Salary, Wage, Acquire, Bring in, Draw in, Gain, Get, Merit
Pictur	Photo, Photograph, Image, Portrait, Simulacrum
Glass	Can, Mug, Stein Vessel
Biscui	Cookie, Cake, Dumpling, Roll

	What for?, What's up?, Huh?, Whatever
What	
Situatio n	State, Condition, Mode, Posture, Status, Surrounding
Minut	Just a minute, Moment, -arily, Instant, Flash, Jiffy, Shake, Twinkle, Wink
Hour	One hour, 60 minutes

Butter	Margarine, Oleo
Honest	Frank, -ly, Honesty, Respect, Sincere, Sure, Genuine, true, Upright, Just, Right, Conscientious, Scrupulous
Welding	Solder, Fusing metals, Brazing, Glue Gun
Draw	Design, Draft, Drawing, Art, Color

	Celebration, Social, Gathering
Party	
Verse	Scripture, Stanza
Late	Not yet, Tardy, Not done, Delayed, Behind, Belated, Overdue, Unpunctual
Durin	While, As, Meanwhile, Mean time, Amid, Thorough out, Midst

	Reptile, Serpent, Viper
Snake	
Worm	Caterpillar, Larva
Soda pop	Soft drink
Spoon	Soup

And then	So on, So forth, Next
Anytim	Whenever
Rich	Wealthy, Well off, Well to do, Affluent, Moneyed, Opulent
Buy	Purchase, Give money

Rise	Get up, Arise, Stand up, Upspring
Meaning	Imply, Intent, Motive, Intend, Purpose, Signify, Stand for, Design, Intent, Import, Aim, Connoting, Denoting
Ticket	Voucher, Claim check, Carte d' entrée, Fine
Write	Scribble, Jot down, Scribe, Correspond, Engross, Inscribe

	Drugs, Medication
Medicine	
Grav	Grease
Throug	Via, Passage, By way of
Escap	Get away, Runaway, Flee, Exit, Evade, Retreat, Bold, Bail out, Abscond, Break, Decamp Lam, Slip

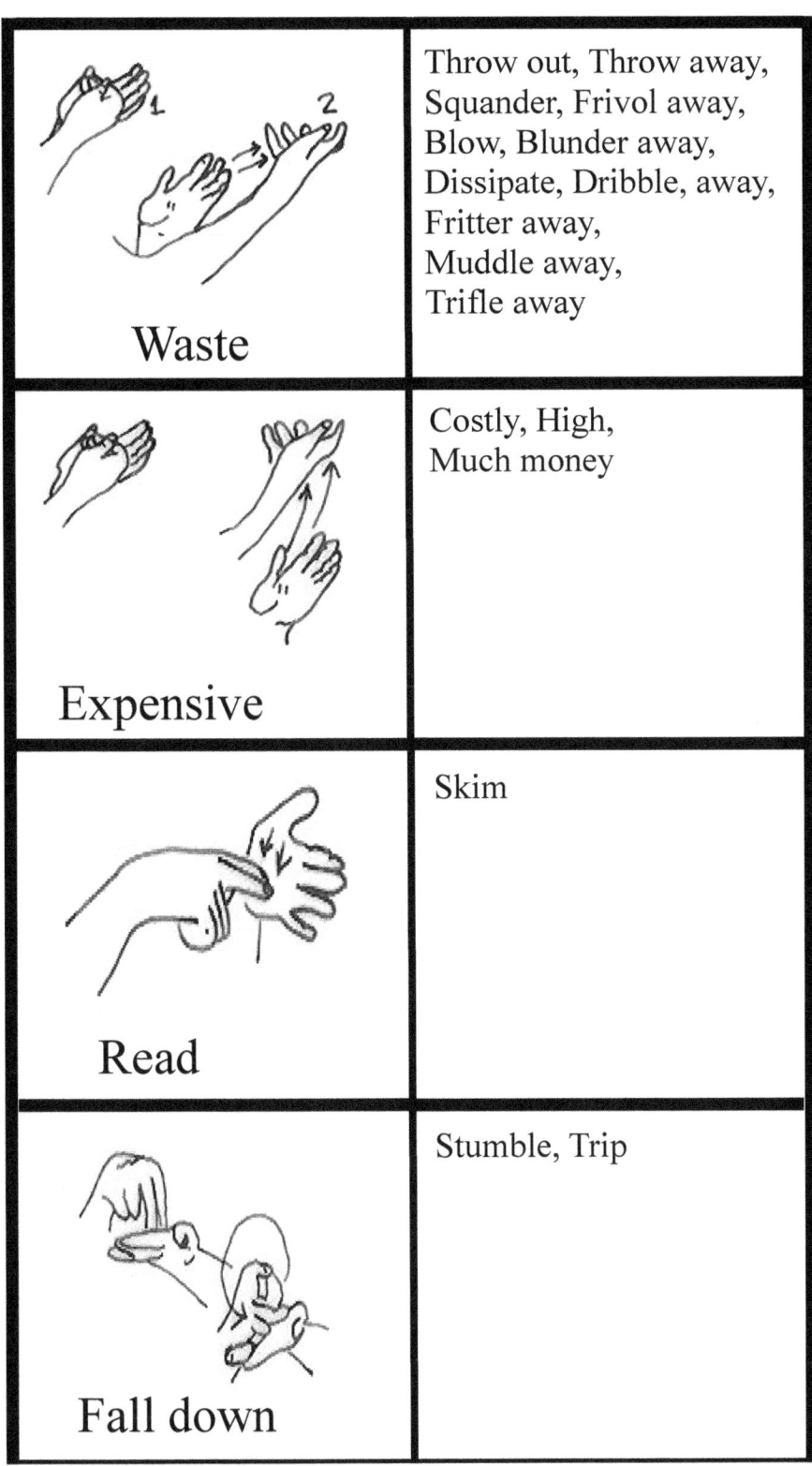

Waste	Throw out, Throw away, Squander, Frivol away, Blow, Blunder away, Dissipate, Dribble, away, Fritter away, Muddle away, Trifle away
Expensive	Costly, High, Much money
Read	Skim
Fall down	Stumble, Trip

Begi ‖	Alpha, Start, Commence, Onset, Initiate, Embark on, Inaugurate, Kick off, Launch, Originate
Mel ι	Dwindle, Vanish, Disappear, Fade, Evaporate, Liquefy, Deliquesce, Flux, Evanesce, Biodegrade, Thaw, Vanish
Smooth	Silky, Glazed, Polished, Sleek, Slick, Refine, Without problems
Pregnant	With child, Expecting, Enceinte, Expectant, Parturient

To	Toward, Goal
Abou	Around, Nearly, Almost, As good as, Approximately, Just about, More or less, Much, Nigh, Practically, Roughly, Roundly
ι **Around**	Surrounding, Neighboring, Round about, Circa, Close on, Nearby
Harvest	Reap, Gather, Collect, Earn, Garner, Ingather, Crop

Plant	Deposit, Sow, Seed
Place (to	Set, Lay, Stick
Monke v	Gorilla, Ape, Orangutan, Chimpanzee, Chimp
Bea	Grizzly, Panda, Teddy

Turtle	Tortoise
Hid	Cover up, Camouflage, Conceal, Ensconce, Stash
Fountain	Spring, Wellspring
Sew	Stitch, Mend

Bring	Carry, Convey, Transport
Plan	Budget, Animus, Arrange, Intend, Intention, Schedule, Scheme, Design
Boa	Barge, Vessel, Ferry, Canoe
Maybe	Possibly, Perhaps, Perchance, Conceivably, Possibly

River	Canal, Creek, Stream
Way	Mode, Passage, Path, Route, Style, Method, Fashion, Manner, Modus, Technique
Road	Street, Avenue, Alley, Lane, Blvd, Highway, Path, Way, Thoroughfare, Track, Sidewalk
Bury	Funeral, Entomb, Inhume, Sepulcher, Sepulture, Tomb

143

	Except, However, Still, Yet, Apart from, Aside from, Barring, Besides, Excluding, Outside
But	
	Amazing, Outstanding, Dandy, Great, Miraculous, swell, Terrific, Marvelous, Dreamy, Nifty, Super, Hunky-dory, Peachy, Sensational
Wonderful	
	Easy-going, Motionless, Peaceful, Phlegmatic, Sedate, Serene, Still, Tranquil, Undisturbed, Quiet, Hush, Lull, Placid, Untroubled, Collected, Composed, Soothing
Calm	
	Direct, Escort, Precede, Conduct, Pilot, Steer
Lea	

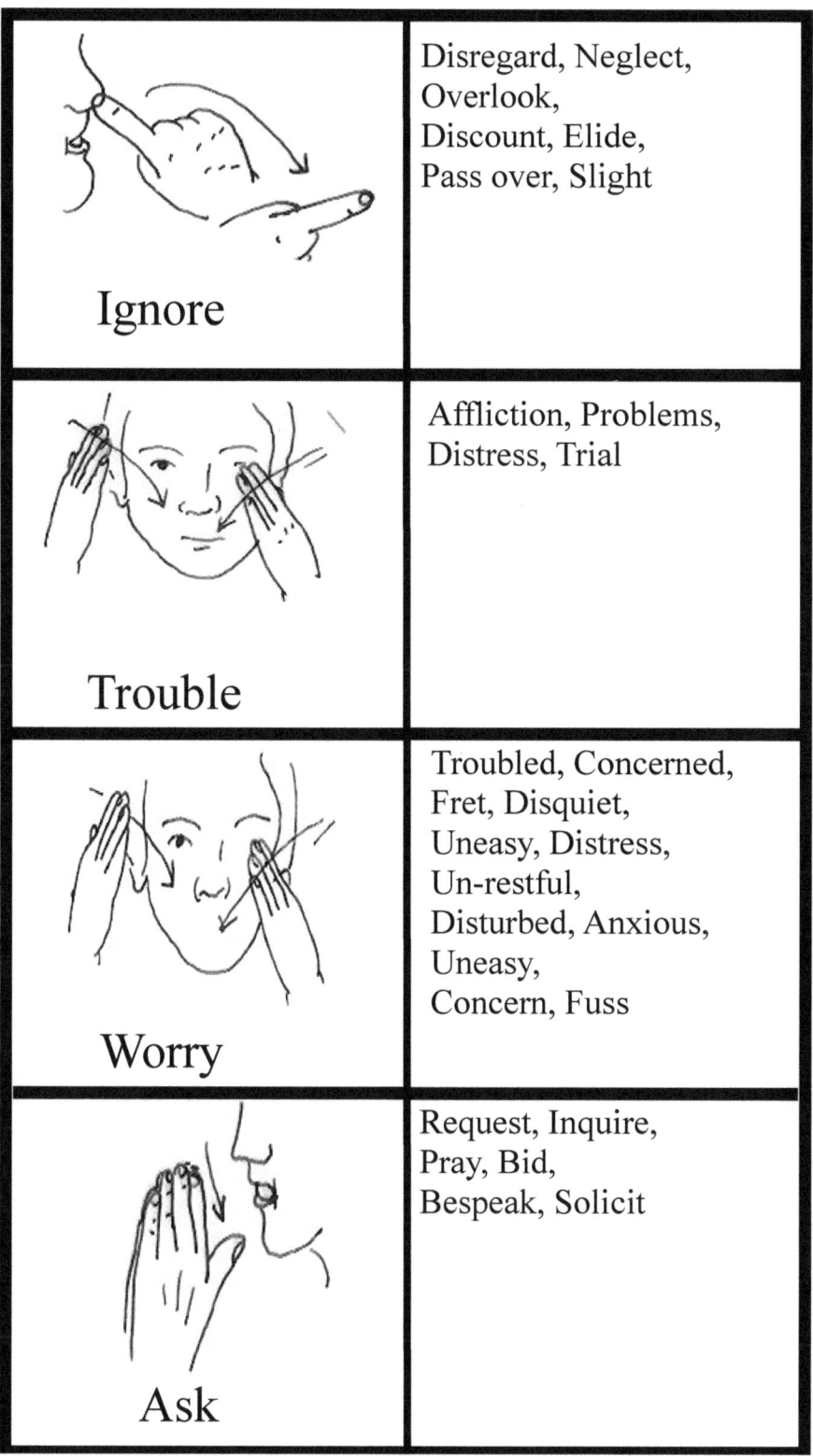

| | Disregard, Neglect, Overlook, Discount, Elide, Pass over, Slight |
| Ignore | |

| | Affliction, Problems, Distress, Trial |
| Trouble | |

| | Troubled, Concerned, Fret, Disquiet, Uneasy, Distress, Un-restful, Disturbed, Anxious, Uneasy, Concern, Fuss |
| Worry | |

| | Request, Inquire, Pray, Bid, Bespeak, Solicit |
| Ask | |

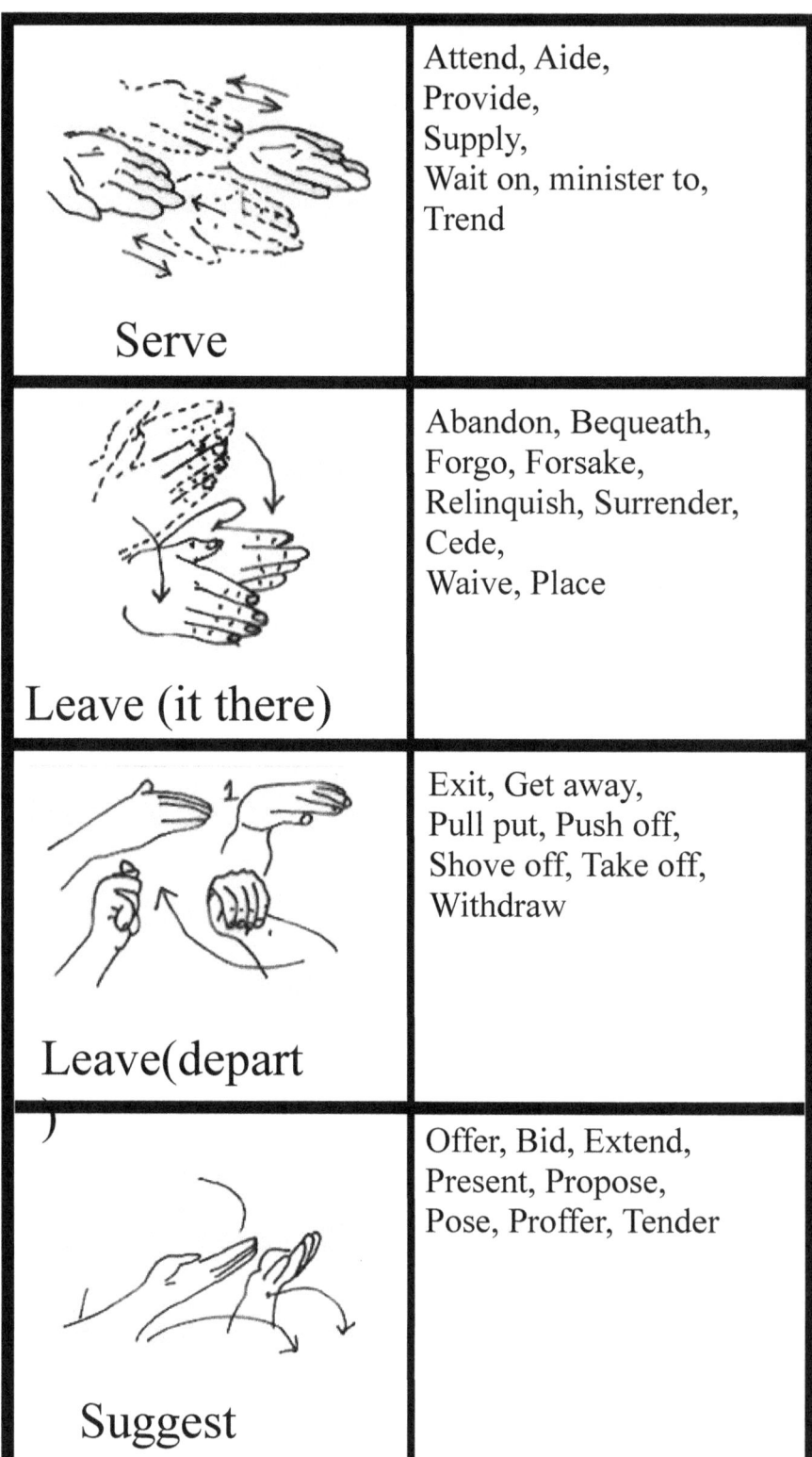

Serve	Attend, Aide, Provide, Supply, Wait on, minister to, Trend
Leave (it there)	Abandon, Bequeath, Forgo, Forsake, Relinquish, Surrender, Cede, Waive, Place
Leave(depart)	Exit, Get away, Pull put, Push off, Shove off, Take off, Withdraw
Suggest	Offer, Bid, Extend, Present, Propose, Pose, Proffer, Tender

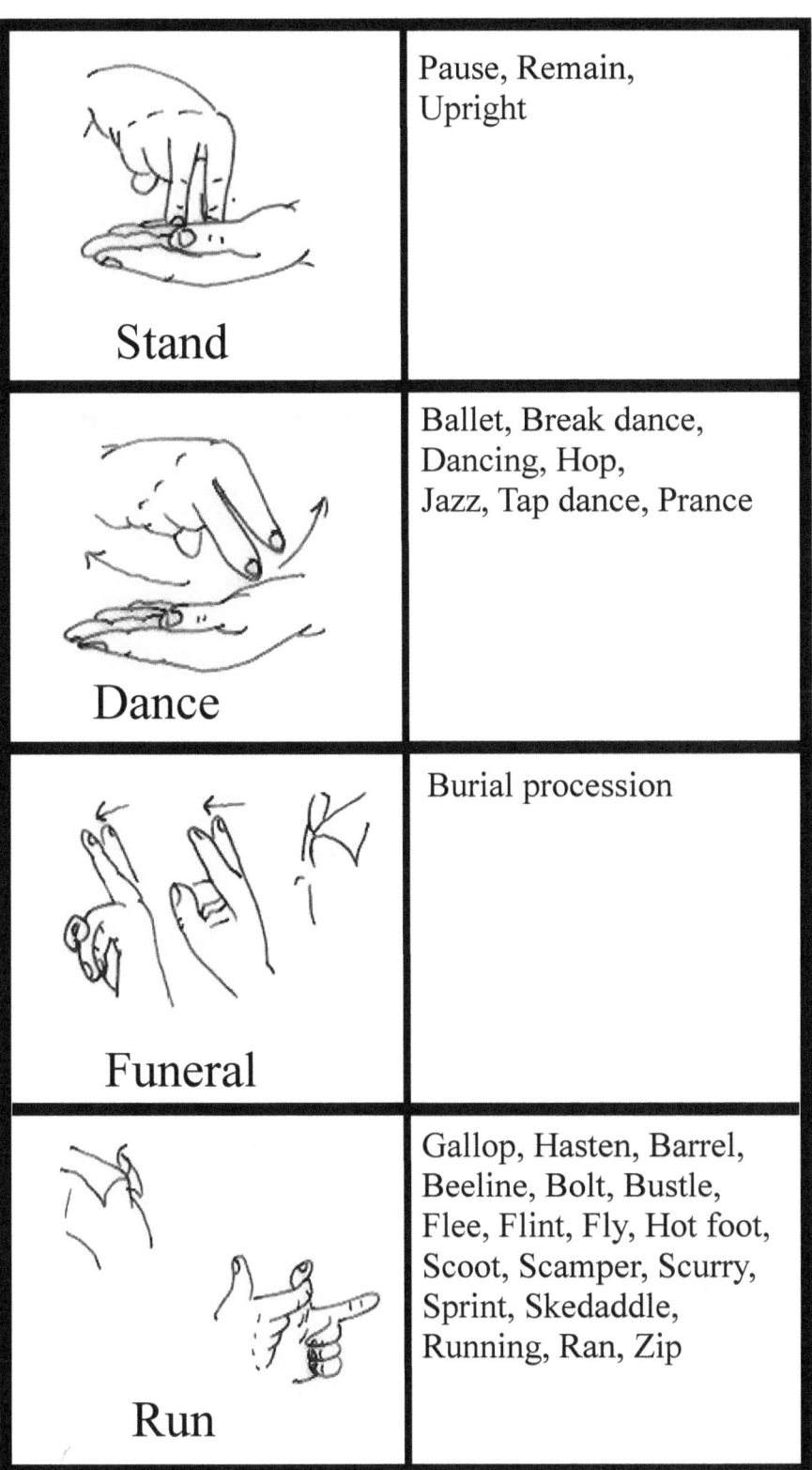

Stand	Pause, Remain, Upright
Dance	Ballet, Break dance, Dancing, Hop, Jazz, Tap dance, Prance
Funeral	Burial procession
Run	Gallop, Hasten, Barrel, Beeline, Bolt, Bustle, Flee, Flint, Fly, Hot foot, Scoot, Scamper, Scurry, Sprint, Skedaddle, Running, Ran, Zip

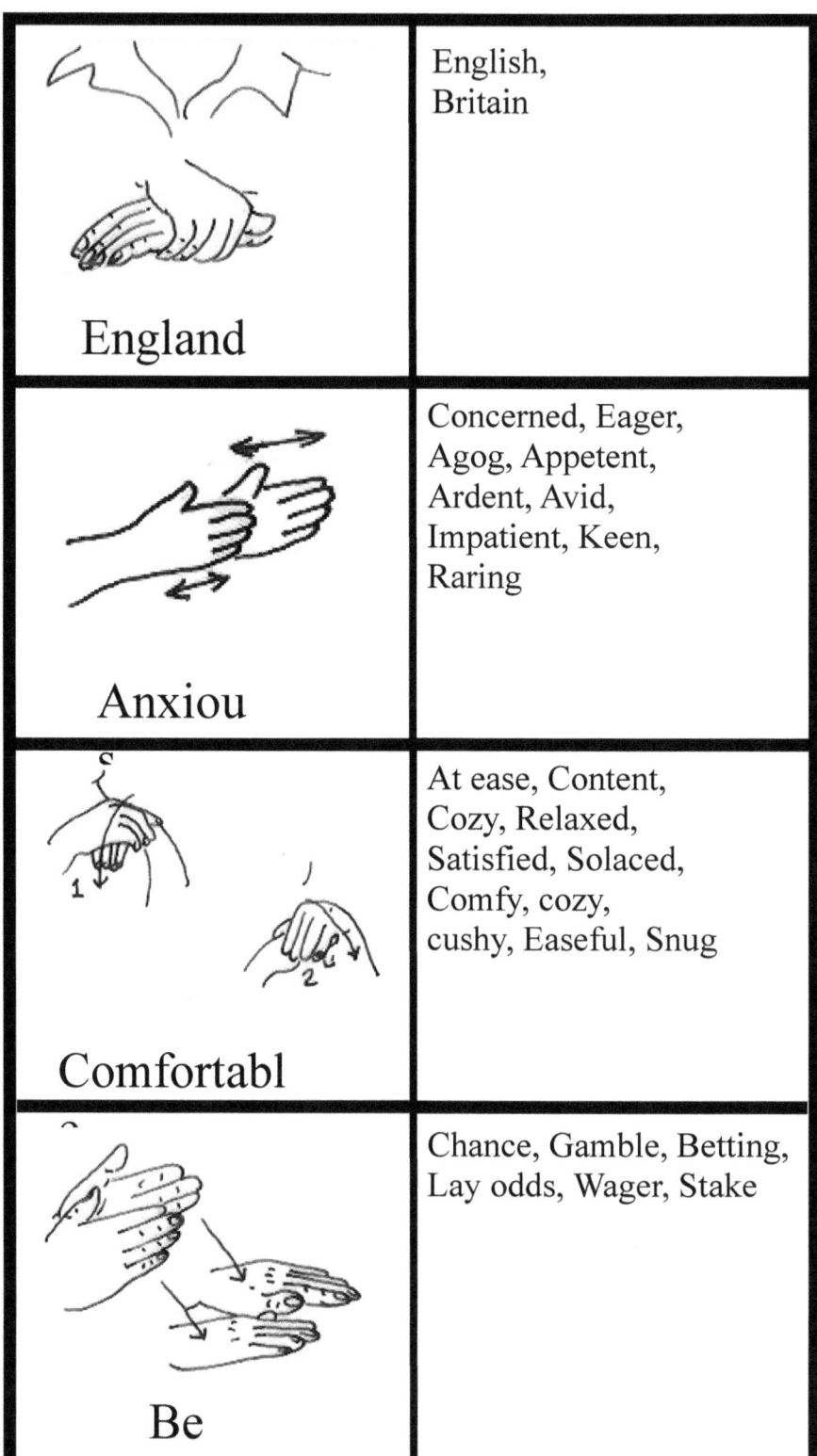

	English, Britain
England	
	Concerned, Eager, Agog, Appetent, Ardent, Avid, Impatient, Keen, Raring
Anxiou	
	At ease, Content, Cozy, Relaxed, Satisfied, Solaced, Comfy, cozy, cushy, Easeful, Snug
Comfortabl	
	Chance, Gamble, Betting, Lay odds, Wager, Stake
Be	

Feet	Foot
Walk	Hike, Meander, Pace, Stroll, Tramp, Tread, Trod, Wander, Ambulate, Foot it, Hoof it, Step, Traipse, Troop, Ramble, Saunter
March	Parade
Luggage	Bag, Baggage, Suitcase

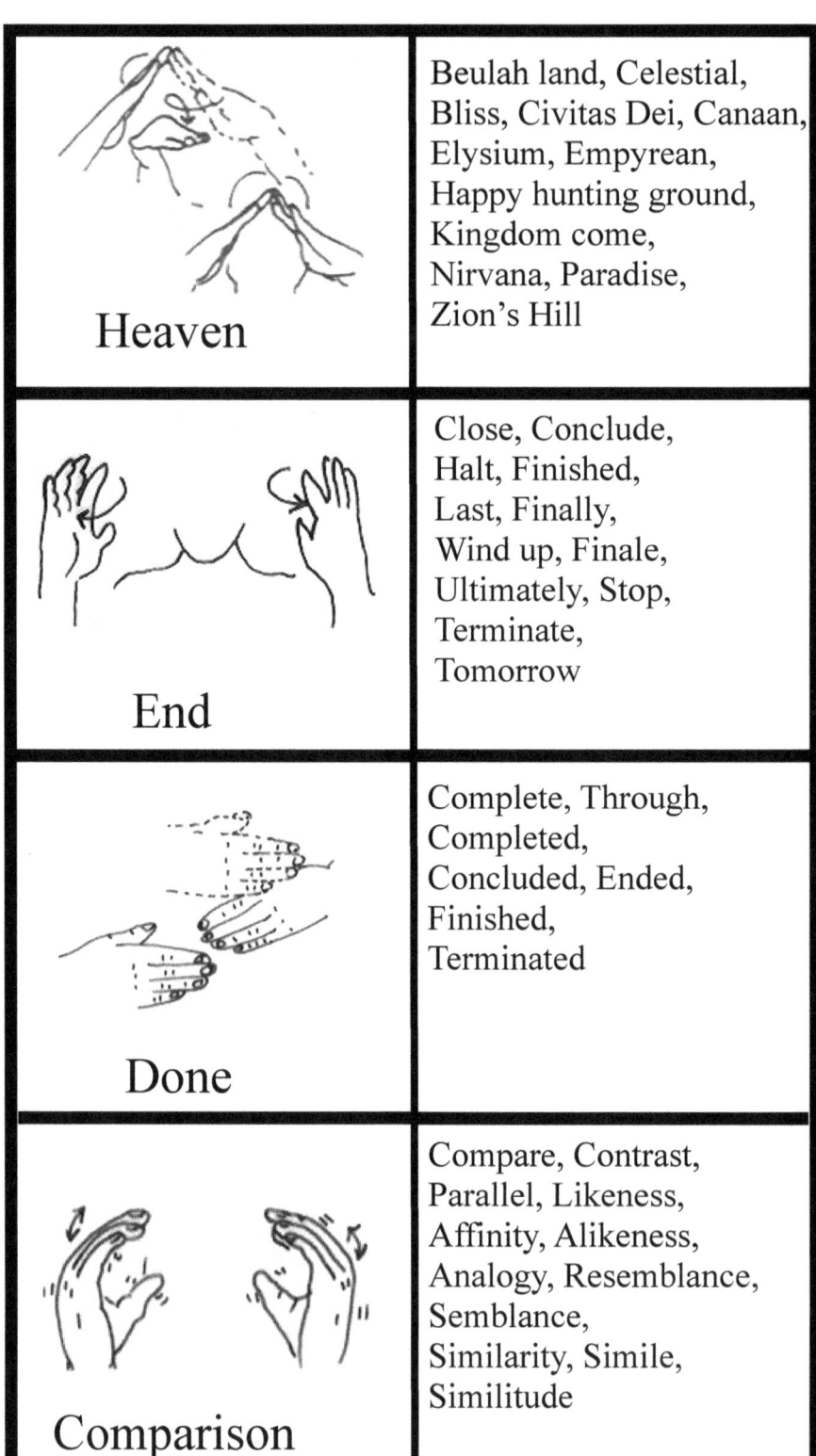

Heaven	Beulah land, Celestial, Bliss, Civitas Dei, Canaan, Elysium, Empyrean, Happy hunting ground, Kingdom come, Nirvana, Paradise, Zion's Hill
End	Close, Conclude, Halt, Finished, Last, Finally, Wind up, Finale, Ultimately, Stop, Terminate, Tomorrow
Done	Complete, Through, Completed, Concluded, Ended, Finished, Terminated
Comparison	Compare, Contrast, Parallel, Likeness, Affinity, Alikeness, Analogy, Resemblance, Semblance, Similarity, Simile, Similitude

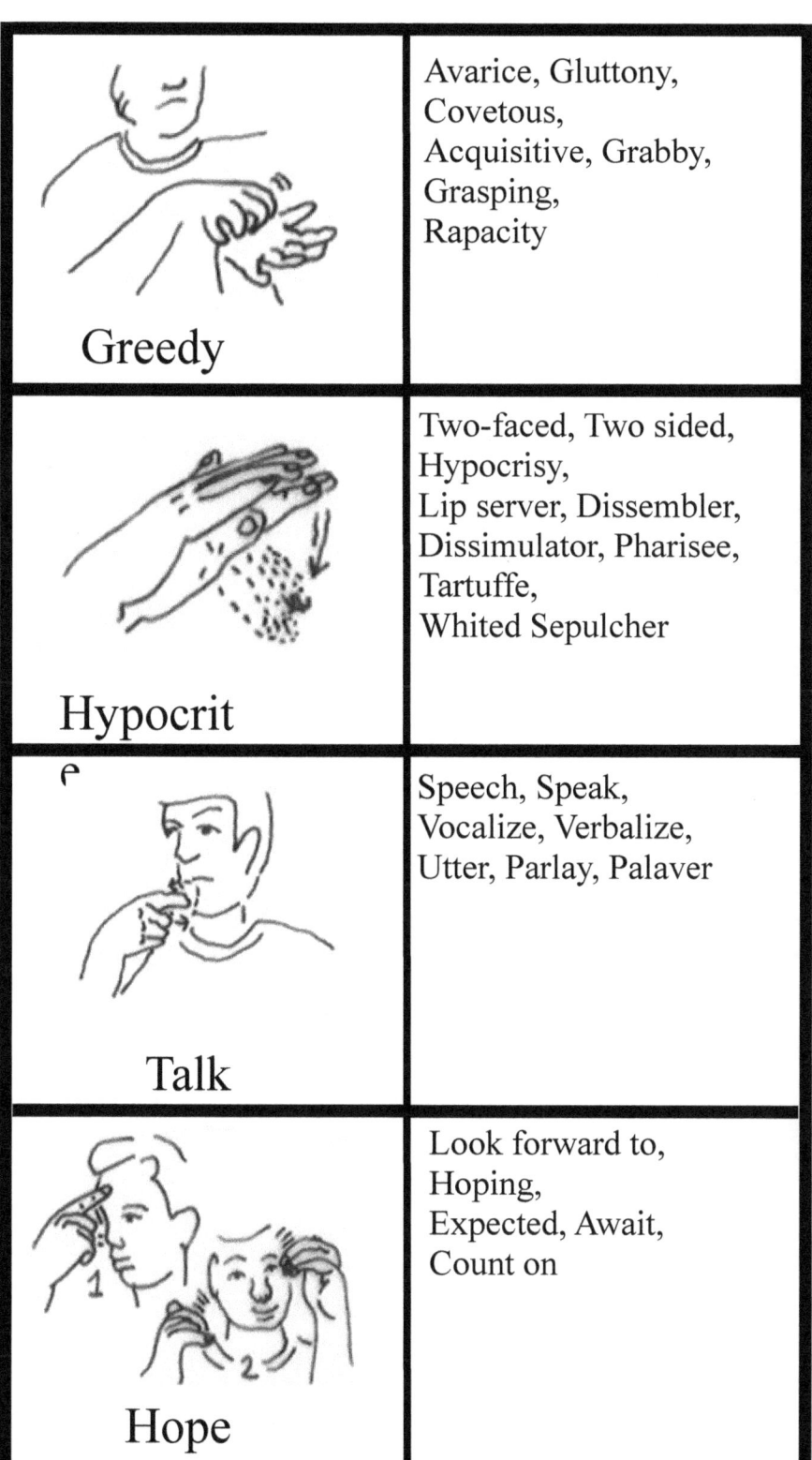

Greedy	Avarice, Gluttony, Covetous, Acquisitive, Grabby, Grasping, Rapacity
Hypocrite	Two-faced, Two sided, Hypocrisy, Lip server, Dissembler, Dissimulator, Pharisee, Tartuffe, Whited Sepulcher
Talk	Speech, Speak, Vocalize, Verbalize, Utter, Parlay, Palaver
Hope	Look forward to, Hoping, Expected, Await, Count on

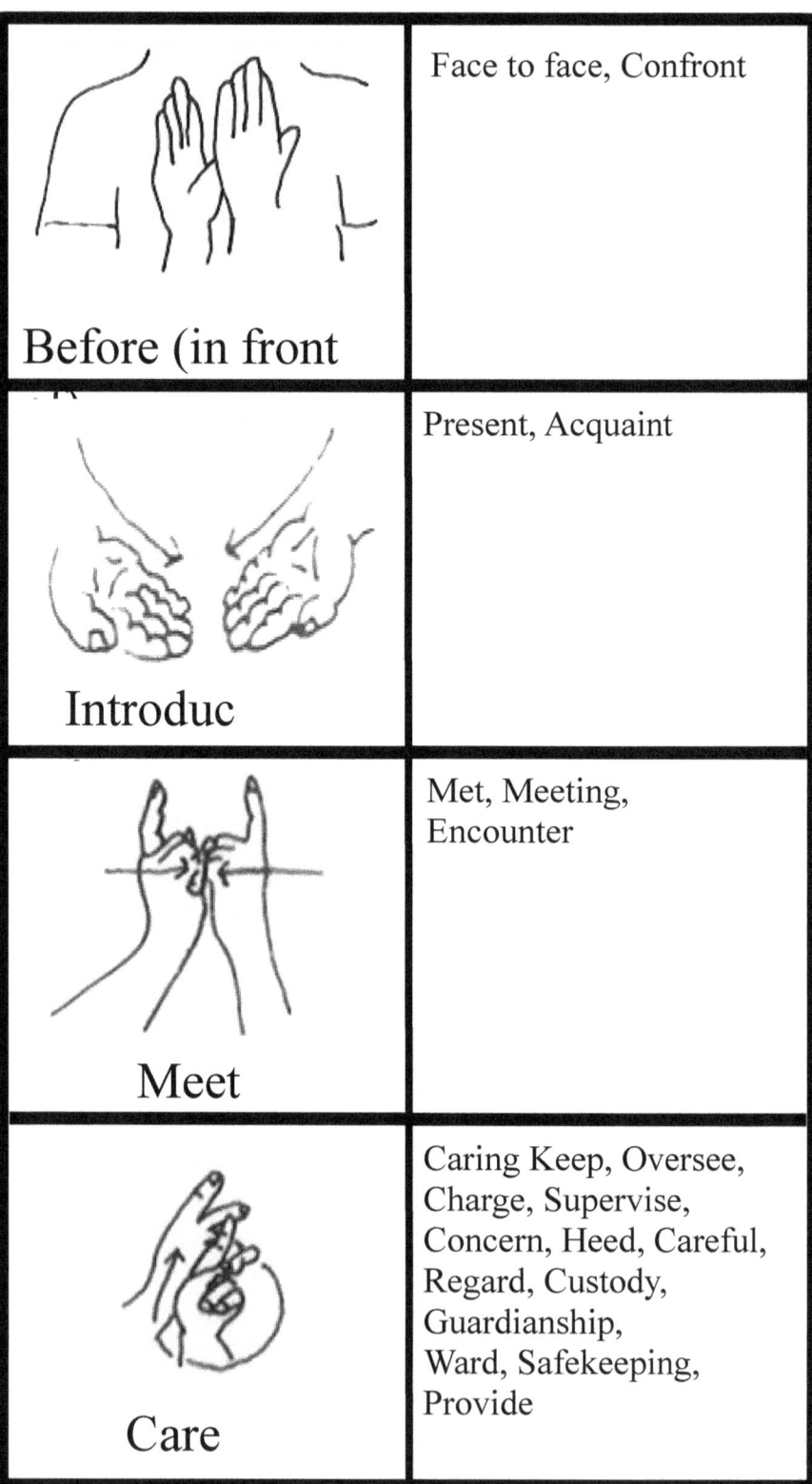 **Before (in front**	Face to face, Confront
Introduc	Present, Acquaint
Meet	Met, Meeting, Encounter
Care	Caring Keep, Oversee, Charge, Supervise, Concern, Heed, Careful, Regard, Custody, Guardianship, Ward, Safekeeping, Provide

Limit	Confines, Bounds, Boundary, Term, Limitation, Restrict
Eage	Desirous, Earnest, Intent, Over anxious, Agog, Anxious, Appetent, Ardent, Athirst, Avid, Breathless, Impatient, Keen, Raring, Solicitous
Nervou s	Anxiety, Jittery, Jumpy, Nervousness, Fidgety, Goosey, High-strung, Nervy, Un-restful
Heavenly Father	Great Father

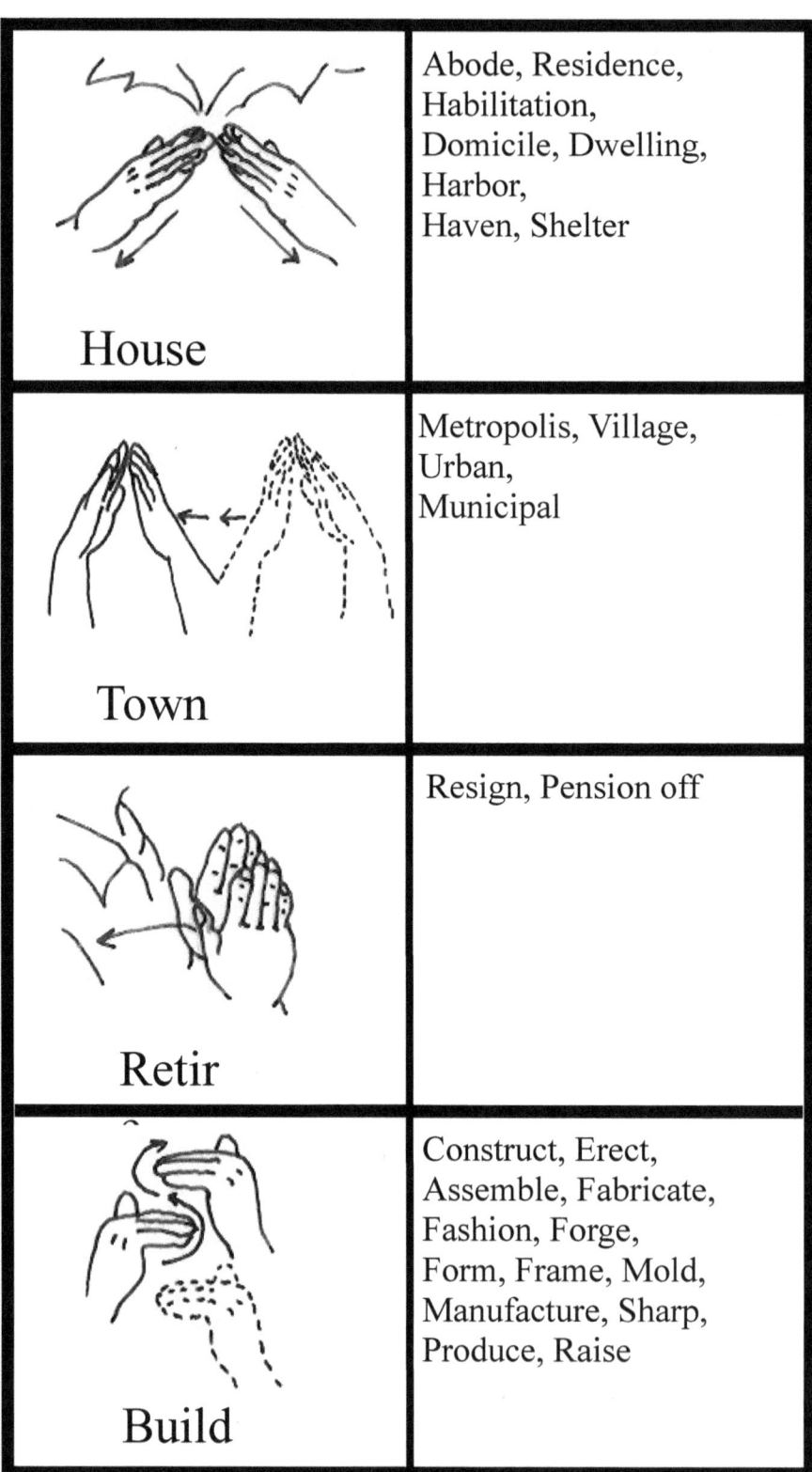

House	Abode, Residence, Habilitation, Domicile, Dwelling, Harbor, Haven, Shelter
Town	Metropolis, Village, Urban, Municipal
Retir	Resign, Pension off
Build	Construct, Erect, Assemble, Fabricate, Fashion, Forge, Form, Frame, Mold, Manufacture, Sharp, Produce, Raise

Above	Aloft, Overhead, O'er
Flat	Even, Flush, Planate, Plane, Smooth
Below	Lower, Under, Underneath
Up to (how far)	To the extent of

Share	Ration, Portion, A lot, Cut, Allotment, Allowance, Apportionment, Quantum
Divide	Distribute, Dichotomize, Split up, Part
After	Beyond, Afterward, Subsequently, Following, Ensuing
Before (time span)	Beforehand, Pre, Previously, Ahead of , Ere, Preceding, Prior to

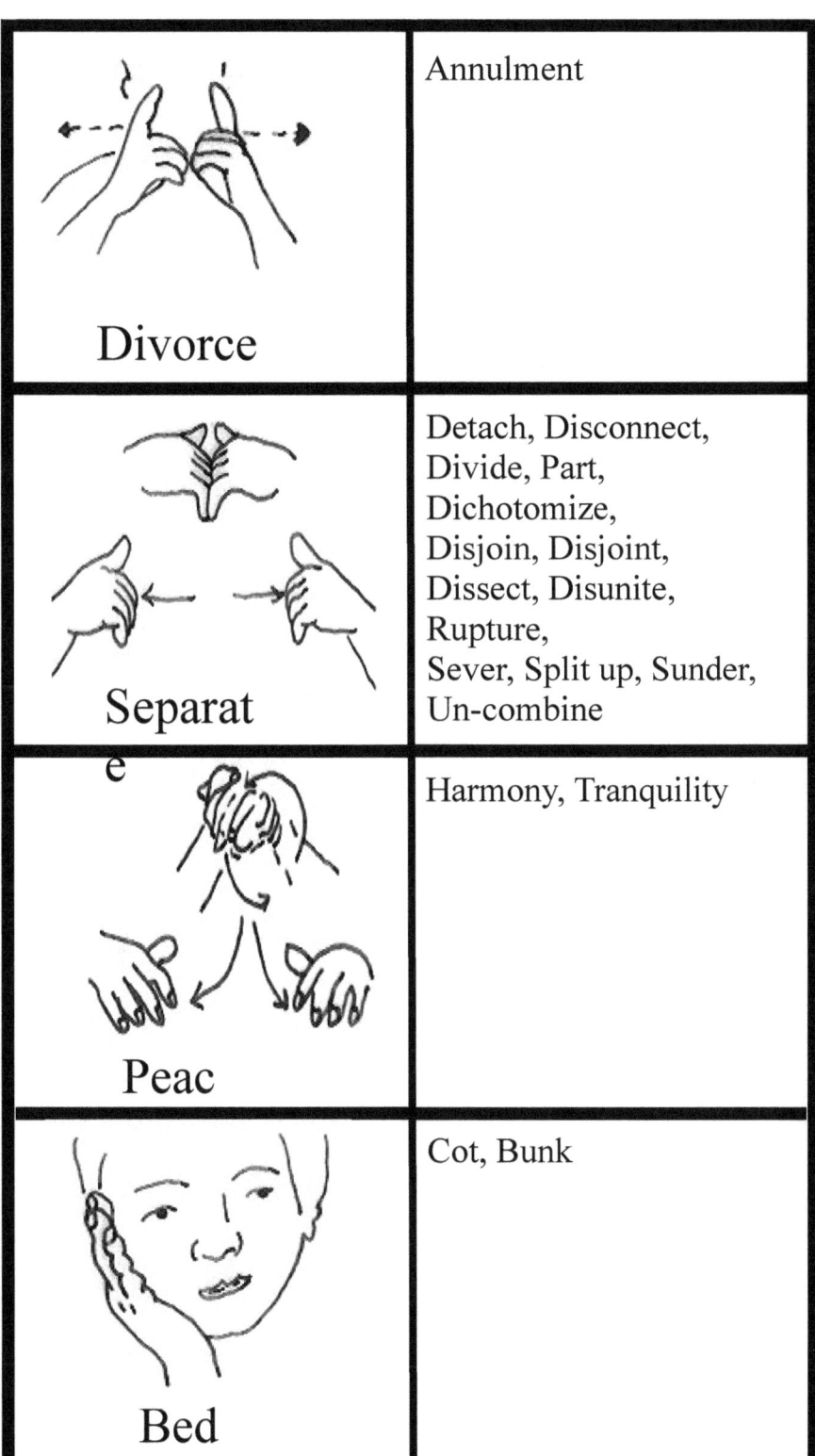

	Annulment
Divorce	
Separate	Detach, Disconnect, Divide, Part, Dichotomize, Disjoin, Disjoint, Dissect, Disunite, Rupture, Sever, Split up, Sunder, Un-combine
Peac	Harmony, Tranquility
Bed	Cot, Bunk

	Ado, Bleak, Bother, Commotion, Complain, Crab, Fret, Gripe, Nag, Quarrel, Squabble, Stir, Squawk, Whimper, Yawp
Fus	
Book	Diary, Portfolio, Journal, Textbook, Novel, Volume, Tome
Christian	Follower of Christ
Jesus	Christ, Yeshiva

Debate	Agitate, Differ, Argumentation Argue, Discuss, Moot, Pro and Con, Trash out, Toss around
Answer	Come back, Come in, Rejoinder, Reply, Respond, Response, Result, Report
Speak	Articulate, Converse, Say, Talk, Utter, Verbalize, Vocalize, Voice
Knife	Blade, Cutlery

Dog	Bow wow, Canine, Hound, Pooch, Pup, Puppy
Pick on	Nag, Henpeck
Champion	Blue Ribbon, First place,
Word	Term

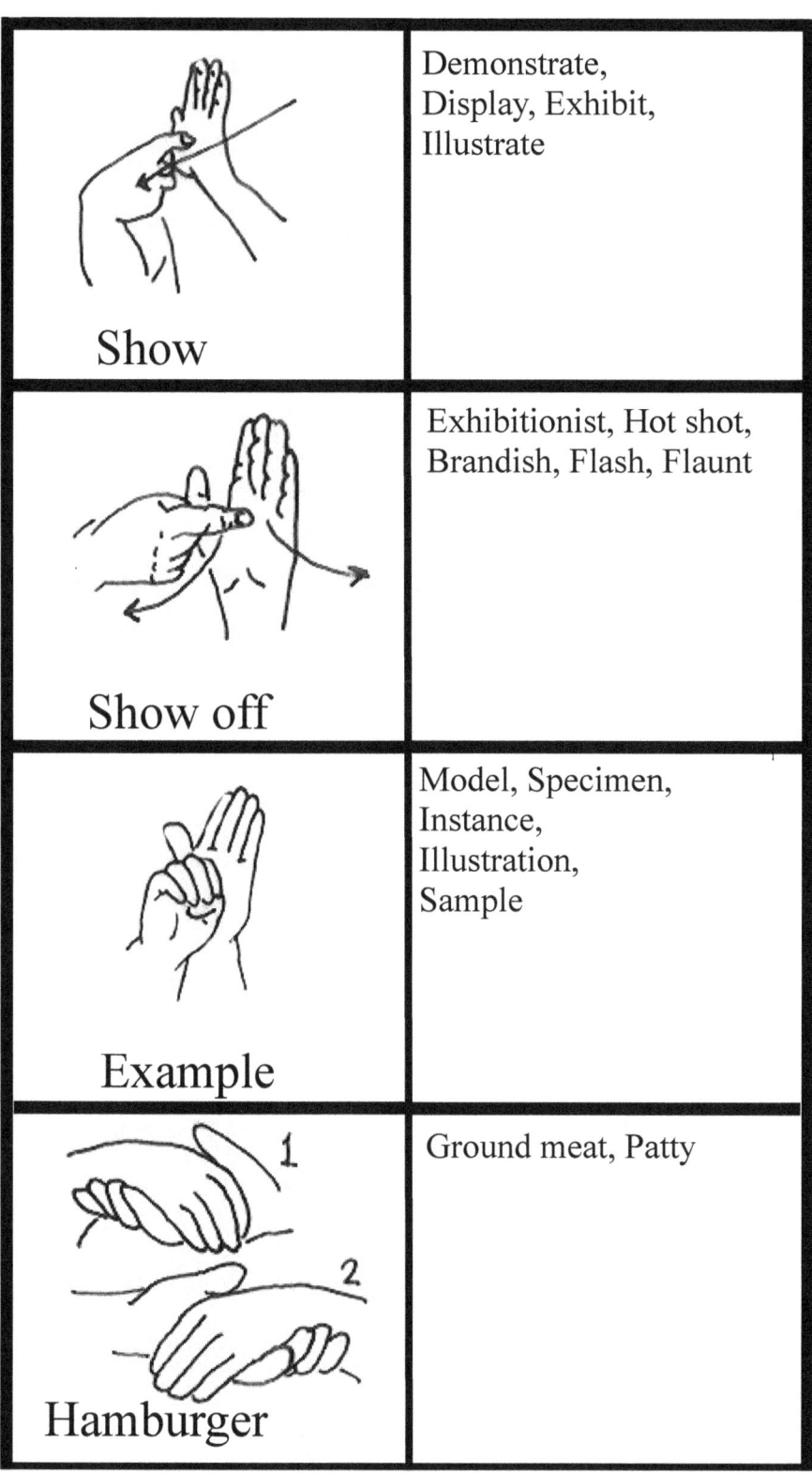

Show	Demonstrate, Display, Exhibit, Illustrate
Show off	Exhibitionist, Hot shot, Brandish, Flash, Flaunt
Example	Model, Specimen, Instance, Illustration, Sample
Hamburger	Ground meat, Patty

	Feline, Kitty, Pussycat
Cat	
	Gentle, Lenient, Malleable, Mild, Mushy, Silky, Smooth, Velvety
Soft	
	Adhesive, Tacky, Gooey, Gluey, Gummy
Sticky	
	Premature
Early	

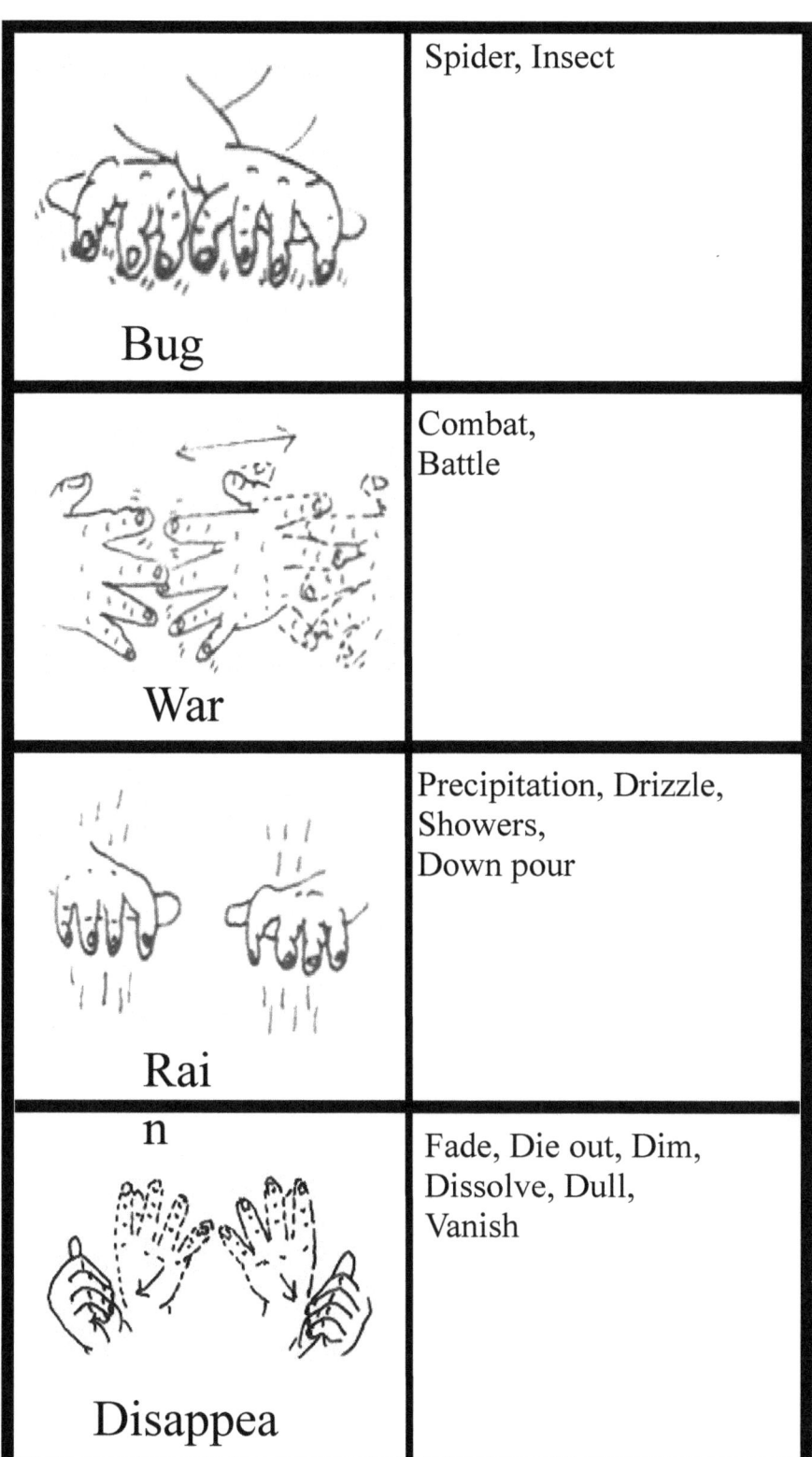

	Spider, Insect
Bug	
War	Combat, Battle
Rai n	Precipitation, Drizzle, Showers, Down pour
Disappea	Fade, Die out, Dim, Dissolve, Dull, Vanish

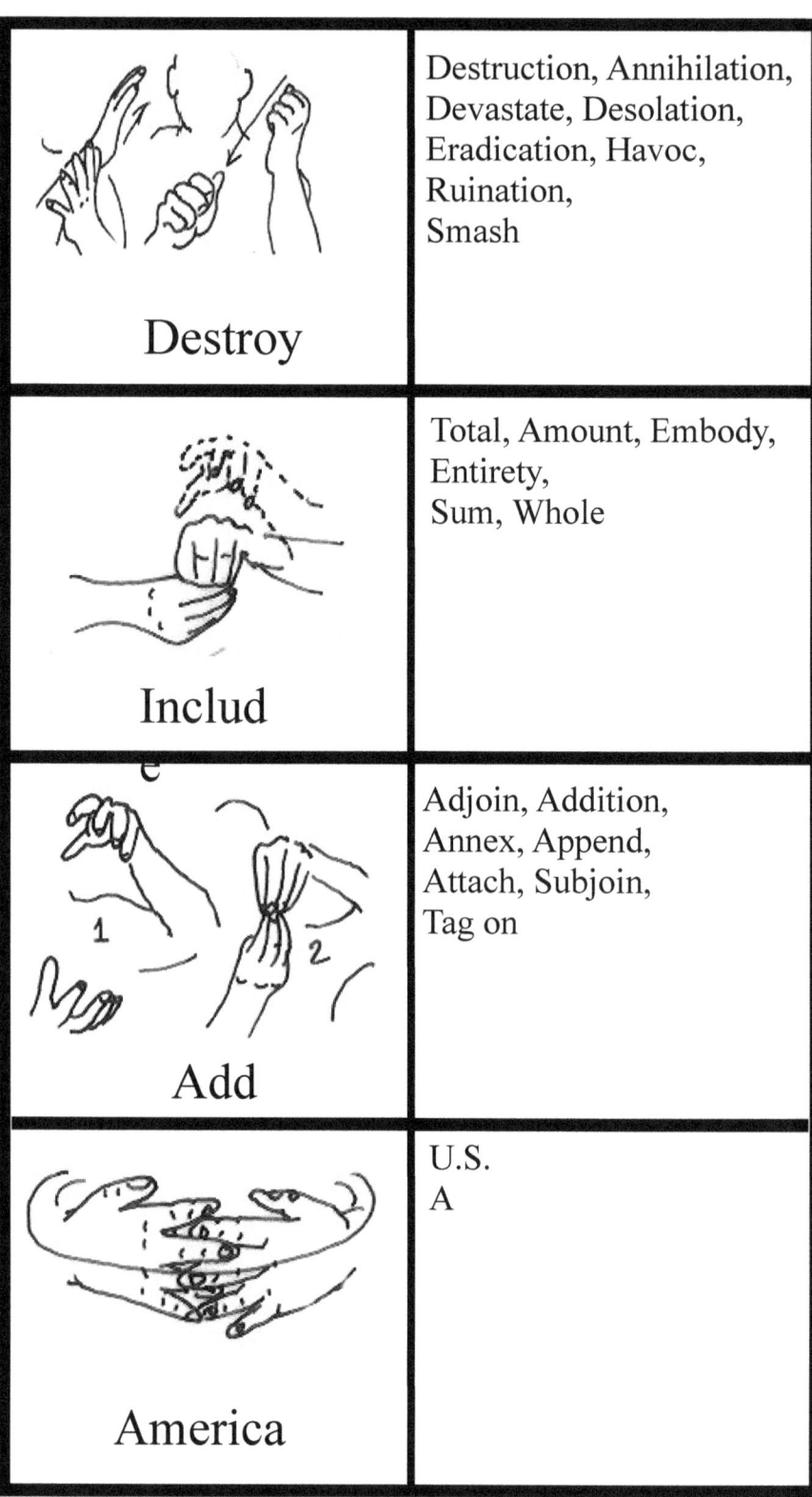

Destroy	Destruction, Annihilation, Devastate, Desolation, Eradication, Havoc, Ruination, Smash
Include	Total, Amount, Embody, Entirety, Sum, Whole
Add	Adjoin, Addition, Annex, Append, Attach, Subjoin, Tag on
America	U.S.A

 Freeze	Paralyze, Petrify, Not move, Stop, Ice
 Piano	Keyboard
 Wait	Linger, Try
 Assume	Take up

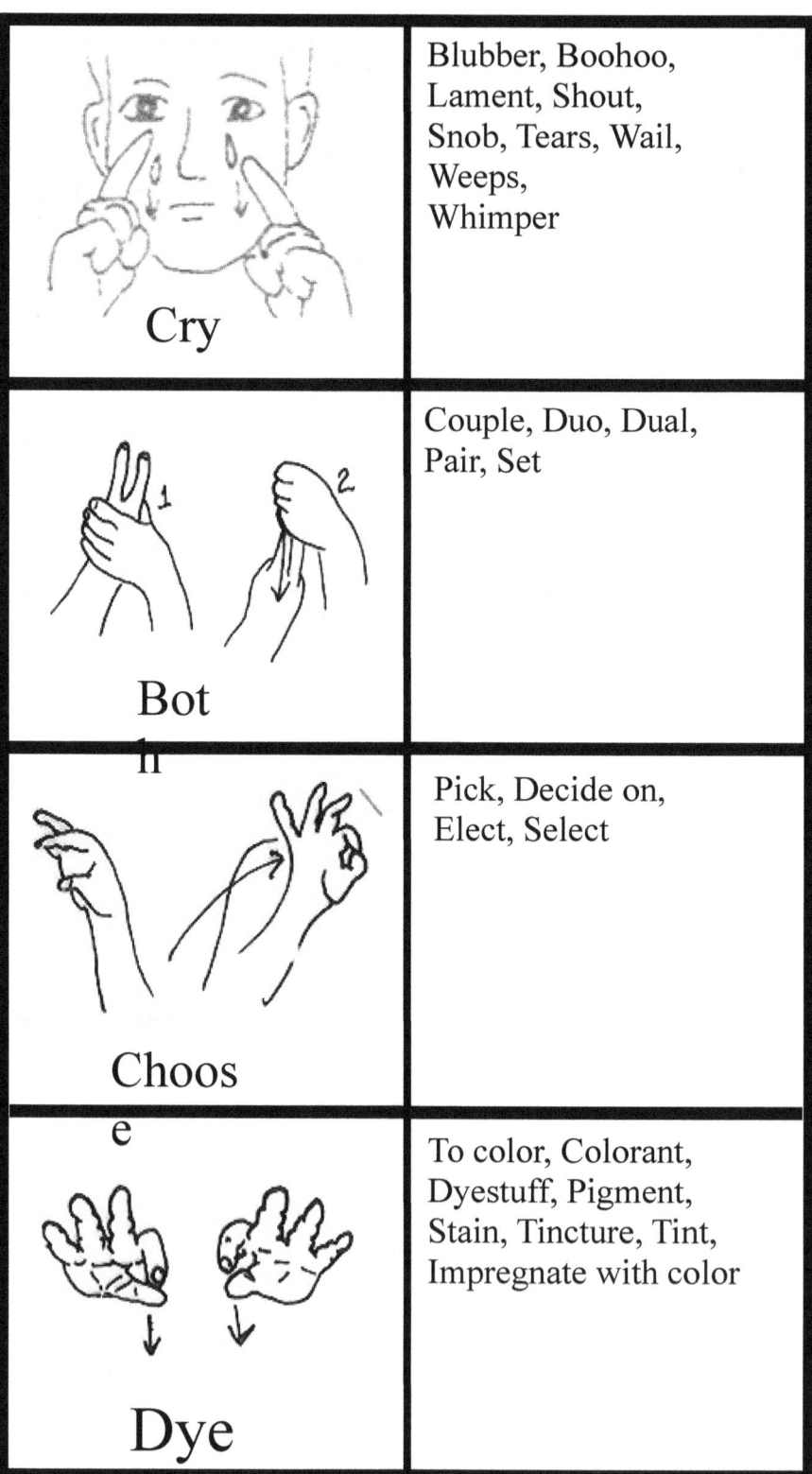

	Blubber, Boohoo, Lament, Shout, Snob, Tears, Wail, Weeps, Whimper
Cry	
Bot h	Couple, Duo, Dual, Pair, Set
Choos e	Pick, Decide on, Elect, Select
Dye	To color, Colorant, Dyestuff, Pigment, Stain, Tincture, Tint, Impregnate with color

Milk	Milk a cow
Alligato	Crocodile, Caiman
Chocolat	Coco a
Where	Everywhere, Location, In what direction?, In what place?, In which position?, Whereabouts, Wherever, Whither

Ambulance	Emergency vehicle
Dictionary	Glossary, Jargon, Lexicon, Palaver, Terminology, Vocabulary
Dollar	Bill, Buck, Legal tender, Oner
Except	All but, Aside, Apart from, But, Except for, Excluding, Exclusive of, Save

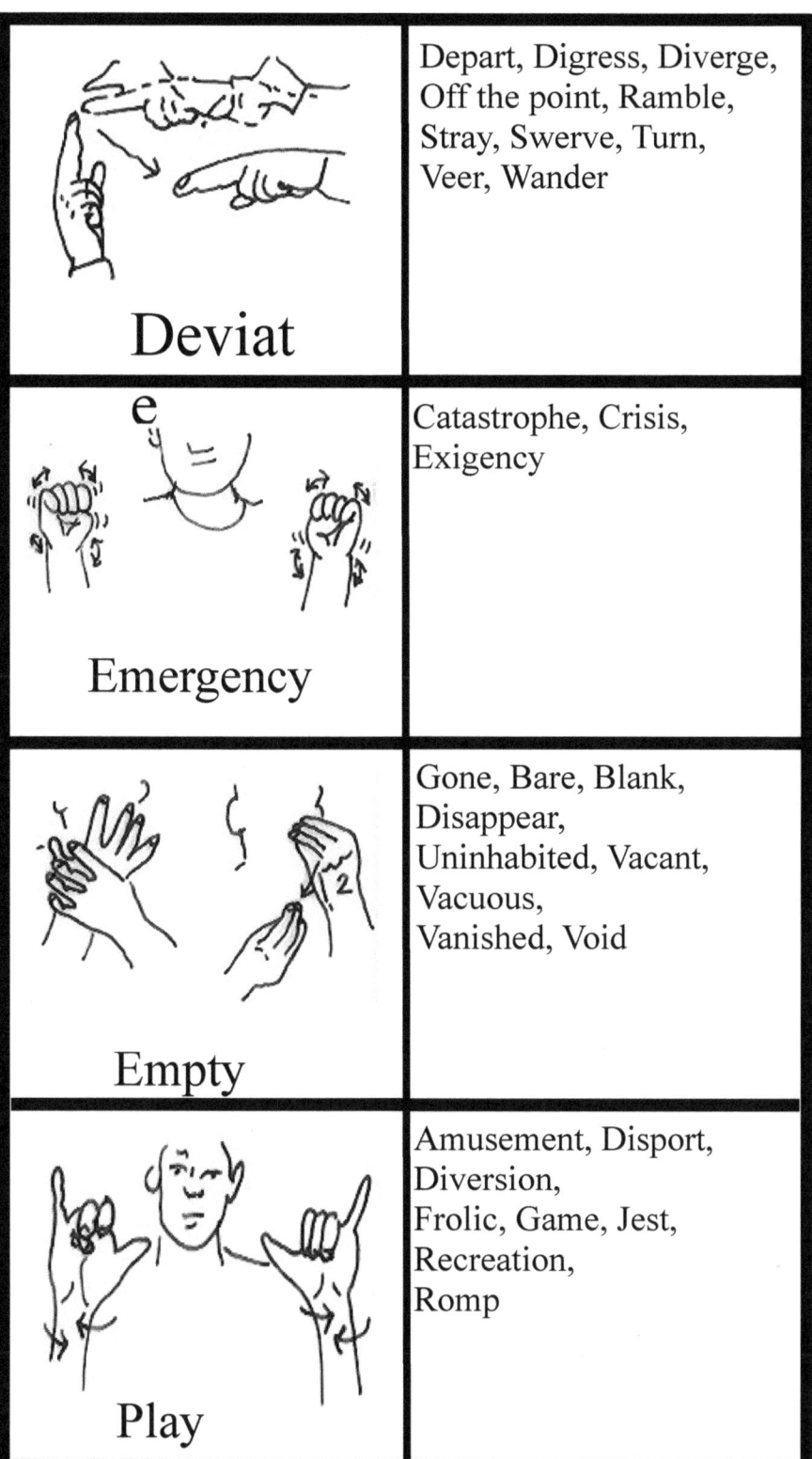	Depart, Digress, Diverge, Off the point, Ramble, Stray, Swerve, Turn, Veer, Wander
Deviate	
Emergency	Catastrophe, Crisis, Exigency
Empty	Gone, Bare, Blank, Disappear, Uninhabited, Vacant, Vacuous, Vanished, Void
Play	Amusement, Disport, Diversion, Frolic, Game, Jest, Recreation, Romp

Si	Iniquity, Transgress, Transgression, Vice, wrong doing
Agren	Accord, Accommodate, Admit, Acknowledge, Assent, Accede, Consist Acquiescence, Cohere, Coincide, In concert, Concord, Concur, Conform, Consent, t, Consort, Correspond, Dovetail, Recognize, Comport,
Socke	Woolies, Booties
Stockings	Hose, Hosiery, Nylons, Panty hose

Anchor	Catch, Fashion, Fix, Grappling iron, Moor, Secure
Shame	Contempt, Debase, Discredit, Disesteem, Disfavor, Disgrace, Dishonor, Disrepute, Embarrass, Humble, Humiliate, Mortify, Ignominy, Infamy, Obloquy, Opprobrium, Reproach
Today	At this time, This day, In the present, Now, Presently, On this day
Challenge	Confront, Duel, Competition, Brave, To dare

	Haughty, Big shot
Big headed	
Fantasize	Fantasy, Imagine, Dream, Hallucinate
Invent	Contrive, Concoct, Cook up, Create, Design, Devise, Dream up, Formulate, Hatch up, Innovate,Make up, Originate, Vamp up
Race	Charge, Contest, Competition, Career, Dash, Marathon

Always	All the time, Constantly, Continually, Ever, Continuously, Eternally, Evermore, n perpetuity, Invariably, Perpetually, Regularly, Unceasingly
Eterna	Everlasting, Ageless, Amaranthine, Dateless, Perdurable, Ceaseless, Endless, Immortal, Infinite, Illimitable, Never ending, Unending, Perpetual, Timeless, World without end
Depend	Cleave to, Cling to, Rely on
Table	Board, Plateau, Tableland, Upland

Independent	Autarkic, Autonomous, Self assured, Self contained, Self sufficient, Self supporting, Self sustained
Hall	Corridor, Passage, Passage way
Blanket	Afghan, Comforter, Cover, Coverlet, Quilt, Spread
Com	Brush

Frustrat	Agitated, Baffled, Bilked, Buffaloed, Dashed, Disappointed, Foiled, Irritated, Thwarted
Suffe r	Agonize, Bear, Endure, Tolerate
Dange	Endanger, Harmful, Hazard, Jeopardy, Peril, -ious, Risk, -y, Parlous, Treacherous, Chancy
Same	Like, As, Also, Too, Alike, Exact, Additionally, Common, Consistent, Constant, Duplicate, Equal, Identical, Equivalent, Indistinguishable, Invariable, Selfsame, Similar, Standard, Such, Unchanging, Unfailing

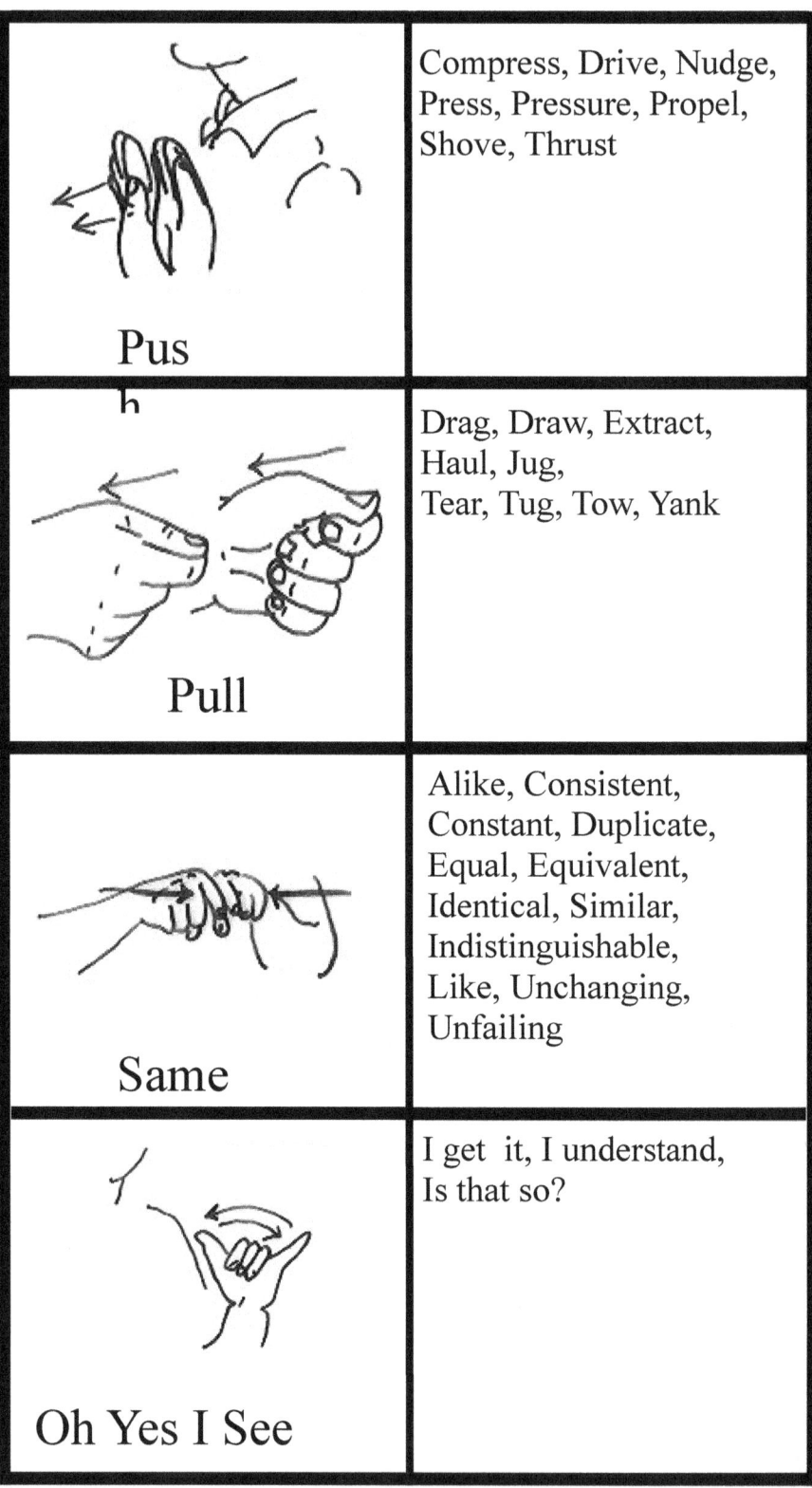

	Compress, Drive, Nudge, Press, Pressure, Propel, Shove, Thrust
Pus h	
Pull	Drag, Draw, Extract, Haul, Jug, Tear, Tug, Tow, Yank
Same	Alike, Consistent, Constant, Duplicate, Equal, Equivalent, Identical, Similar, Indistinguishable, Like, Unchanging, Unfailing
Oh Yes I See	I get it, I understand, Is that so?

 Dow	Below, Downward
 Up	Arise, Ascend, Aspire
 Wrestle	Brawl, Grapple, Scuffle, Struggle, Tangle, Tussle
 Compute	Data processor

	Called, Appoint, Designate, Finger, Nominate, Tap, Give title
Nam	
Hurr	Accelerate, Celerity, Dispatch, Hustle, Hasten, Quicken, Rush, Scamper, Swiften
Rabbit	Bunny, Hare
Borrow	Lend, Loan

Supervise	Monitor, Patrol, Take care of, Oversee, Chaperon, Overlook, Superintend
Plat e	Platter
Rocking chair	Rocker
Giv	Distribute, Hand out, Pass out, Present, Donate, Grant, Provide, Dish out, Deliver, Dispense, Furnish, Supply

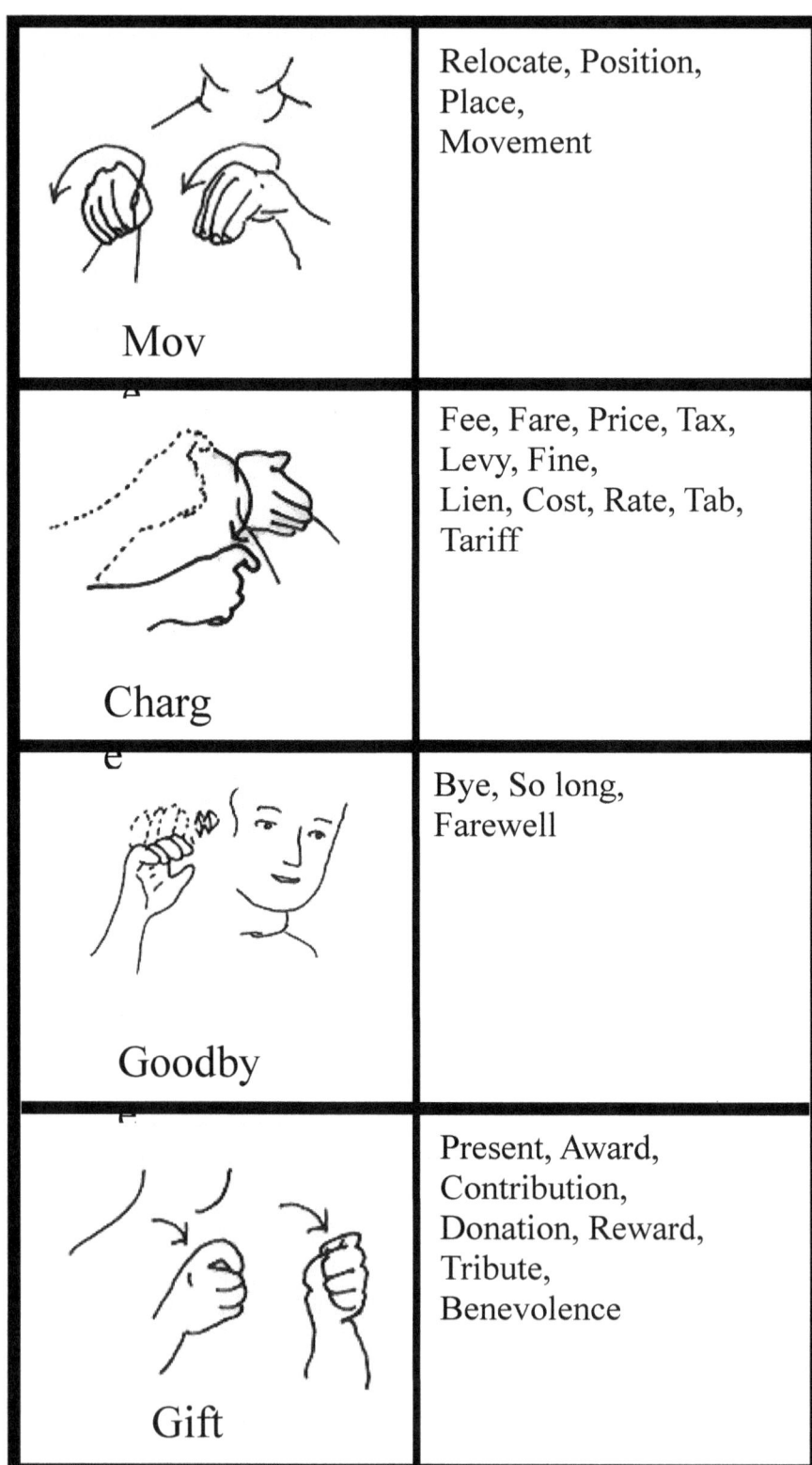

Move	Relocate, Position, Place, Movement
Charge	Fee, Fare, Price, Tax, Levy, Fine, Lien, Cost, Rate, Tab, Tariff
Goodbye	Bye, So long, Farewell
Gift	Present, Award, Contribution, Donation, Reward, Tribute, Benevolence

Le	Allow, Grant, Leave, Permit, Suffer
t **Permissio**	Let, Allow, Permit, Authorize, Consent
People	Folk, Public
Kitchen	Mess Hall, Galley, Dining hall

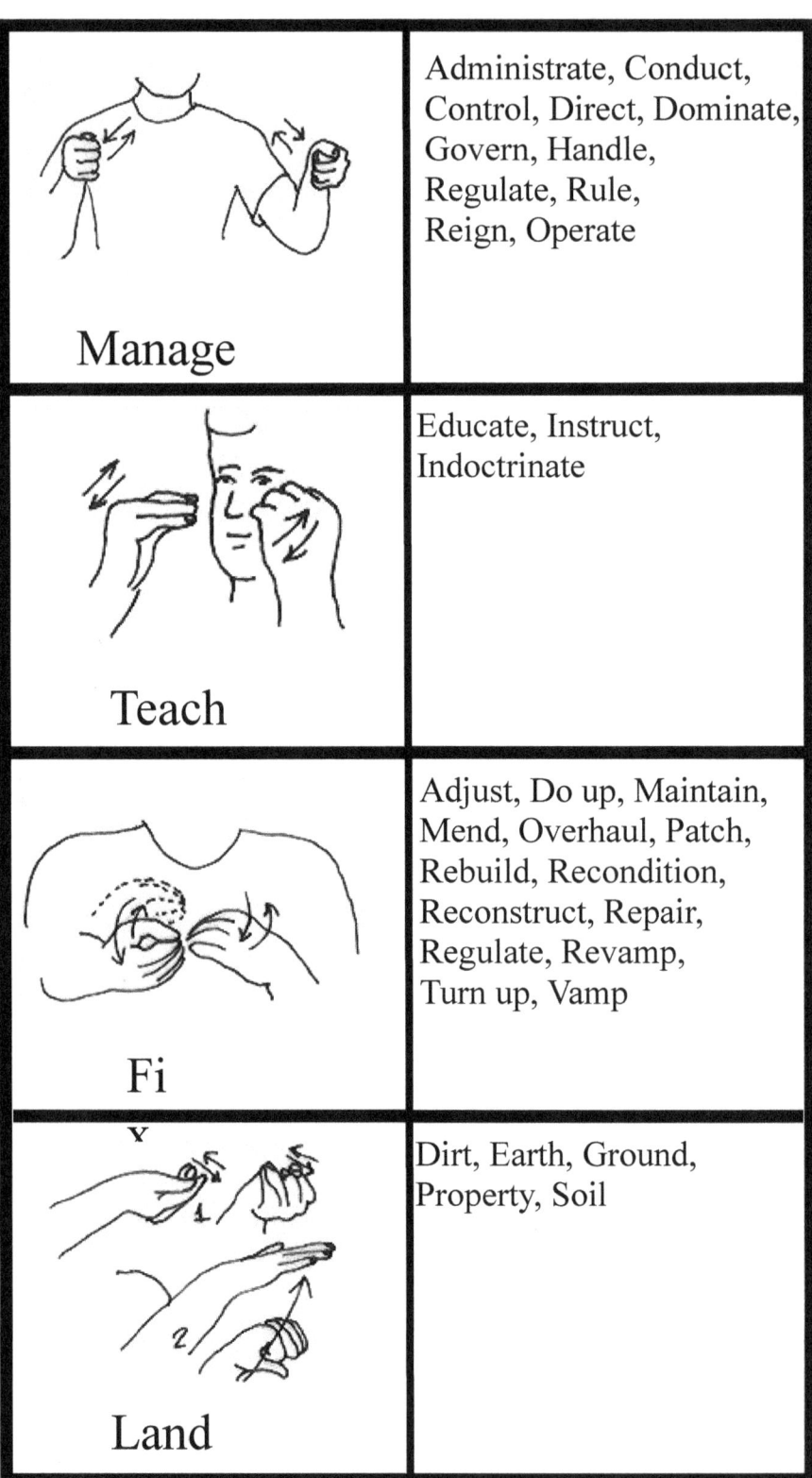

Manage	Administrate, Conduct, Control, Direct, Dominate, Govern, Handle, Regulate, Rule, Reign, Operate
Teach	Educate, Instruct, Indoctrinate
Fi	Adjust, Do up, Maintain, Mend, Overhaul, Patch, Rebuild, Recondition, Reconstruct, Repair, Regulate, Revamp, Turn up, Vamp
Land	Dirt, Earth, Ground, Property, Soil

Spread(tell abroad)	Tell, Declare, Proclaim, Announce, Advertise
Gossip	Blab, Carry tale, Circulator, Gad, Mumble news, Rumor, Rumor monger, Scandalize, Tale bearer, Buzz, Grapevine, Hearsay
Restroom	Toilet, Men's/Ladies room, Lavatory, Washroom, Powder room
Toilet	Commode, Convenience, Head, John, Privy, Johnny, Latrine, Lavatory, Restroom, Water closet

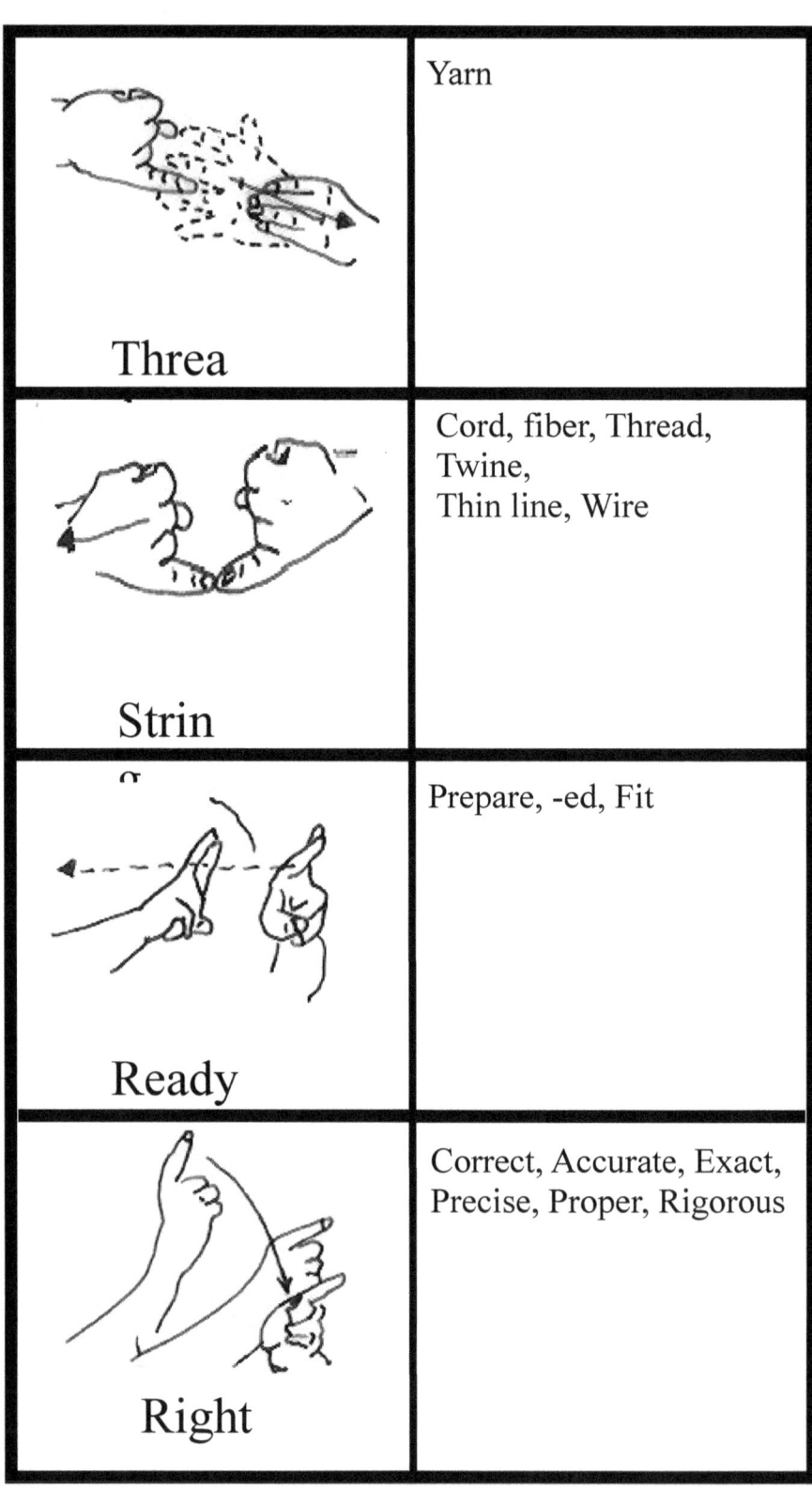

	Yarn
Threa	
Strin	Cord, fiber, Thread, Twine, Thin line, Wire
Ready	Prepare, -ed, Fit
Right	Correct, Accurate, Exact, Precise, Proper, Rigorous

Spread	Circulate, -ed, Diffuse, Dispersed, Disseminate, Distribute, Epidemic, Expand, Extend, Fan out, Outspread, Outstretch, Propagate, Strew, Unfold
Clear	Clarify, Bright, Clarion, Fair, Cloudless, Evident, Fine, Glitter, Glisten, Pellucid, Illuminate, Light, Limpid, Rainless, Shine, Sunny, Lucid Radiant, Translucent, Lucent Transparent, Unclouded, Beaming, Brilliant, Effulgent, Fulgent, Incandescent,
Store	Market, Mart, Outlet, Shop, Showroom
Sell	Market, Merchandise, Peddle, Retail, Vend

Last	Closing, Concluding, End, Final, Finally, Hindmost, Rearmost, Terminal, Ultimate
Bos s	Authority, Chaperon, Chief, Head, Chieftain, Commander, Dominator, Headman, Honcho, Manager, Master, Overlook, Overseer, Quarter back, Superior, Supervise, Supervisor, Superintendent
Self	Yourself, Myself, Himself, Herself
Other	Another, Else, Different, Disparate, Dissimilar, Divergent, Diverse, Otherwise

Can	Capable, May, Able
Can't	Incapable, Unable, Not permitted
Do	Execute, Act
Stay	Abide, Adjourn, Arrest, Bide, Check, Defer, Delay, Fixed, Hold off, Hold over, Hold up, Interrupt, Layover, Linger, remain

Rule	Govern, Reign, Administrate, Preside
Tiny	Little bit, Minute, Microscopic, Diminutive, Itsy-bitsy, Miniature, Pint size, Teensy
Must	Need, Should, Ought, Obligated, Bound, Necessary
United States	U.S.A., America

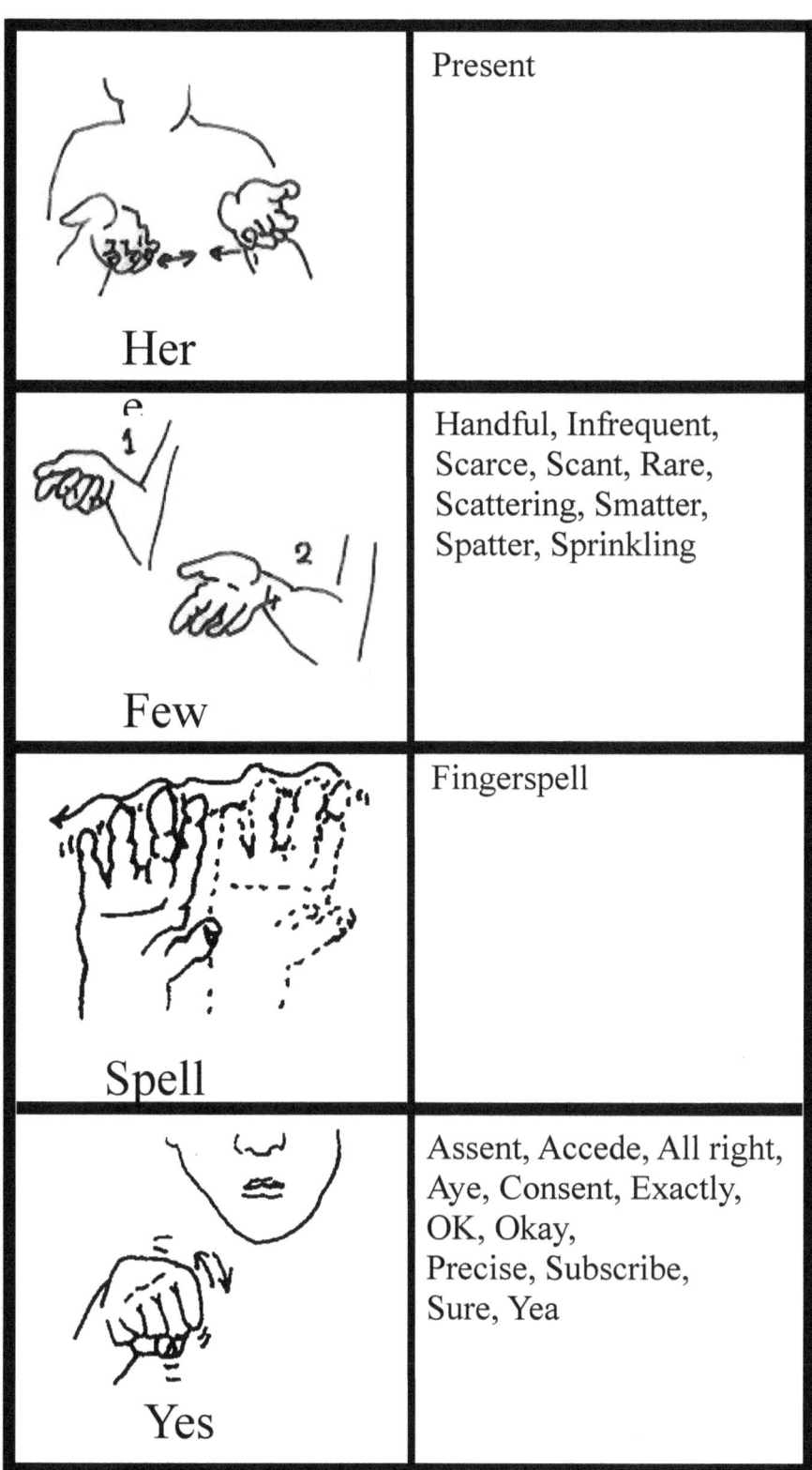

	Present
Her	
Few	Handful, Infrequent, Scarce, Scant, Rare, Scattering, Smatter, Spatter, Sprinkling
Spell	Fingerspell
Yes	Assent, Accede, All right, Aye, Consent, Exactly, OK, Okay, Precise, Subscribe, Sure, Yea

Win	Celebrate, Victory, Jubilee, Triumph, Festival, Conquest, Success, Rejoice, Conquer, Prevail, Overcome
Tie	Neckpiece
Exact	Accurate, Precise, Correct
Perfec	Flawless, Infallible, Impeccable, Faultless, Ideal, Absolute, Fleckless, Indefectible, Unflawed, Model, Unblemished, Unmarred

Continue	Still, Persist, maintain, Endure, Abiding, Lasting
Measure	Gauge, Scale, Size, Dimensions, Magnitude, Proportion
Hate	Despise, Loathe, Abhor, Spite, Malice, Abominate, Aversion, Detest, Disdain, Execrate
Try	Attempt, Undertake, Endeavor, Strive

 Mirror	Reflection, Looking glass, Imager
 Nut(person)	Crackpot, Crazy, Kook, Loon, Ding-a-ling, Harebrain, Screwball
 Governmen t	Administration, Regime
 Mercy	Compassion, Pity, Leniency, Charity, Clemency, Lenity

	Soar, Fly, Aviate
Airplan	
	Adversary, Foe, Opponent, Opposition, Oppose
Enem y	
	Neighbor, Partner, Buddy, Pal, Acquaintance, Amigo, Confidant
Friend	
	Electric
Electricity	

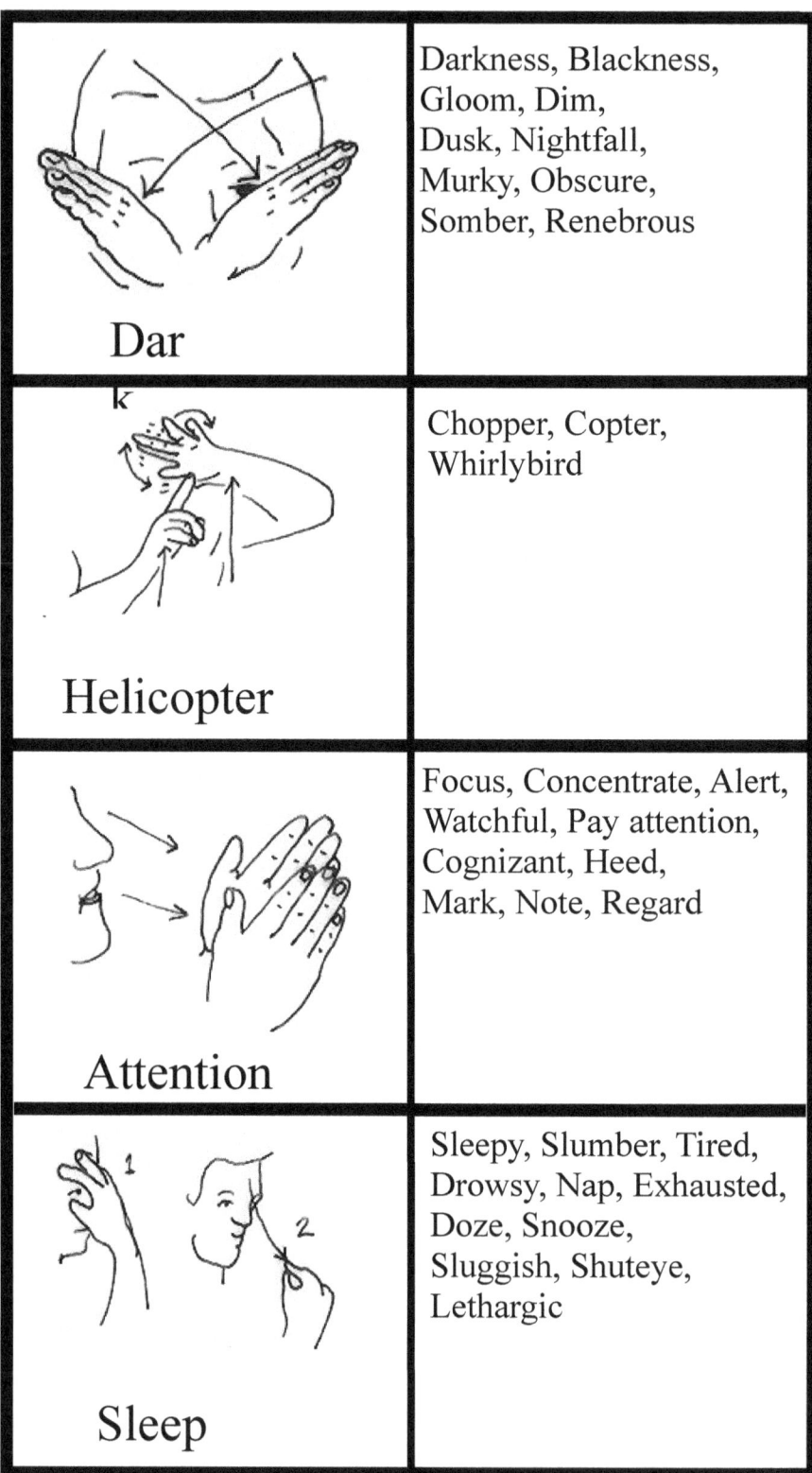

Dar	Darkness, Blackness, Gloom, Dim, Dusk, Nightfall, Murky, Obscure, Somber, Renebrous
Helicopter	Chopper, Copter, Whirlybird
Attention	Focus, Concentrate, Alert, Watchful, Pay attention, Cognizant, Heed, Mark, Note, Regard
Sleep	Sleepy, Slumber, Tired, Drowsy, Nap, Exhausted, Doze, Snooze, Sluggish, Shuteye, Lethargic

Lion	King of the Jungle, King of Beasts
Noise	Clamor, Sound, blare, Racket
Disgusted	Overwrought, Fed up, Had enough, Discontented, Aggravated, Dissatisfied
Blush	Redden, Embarrassed, Flush, Glow

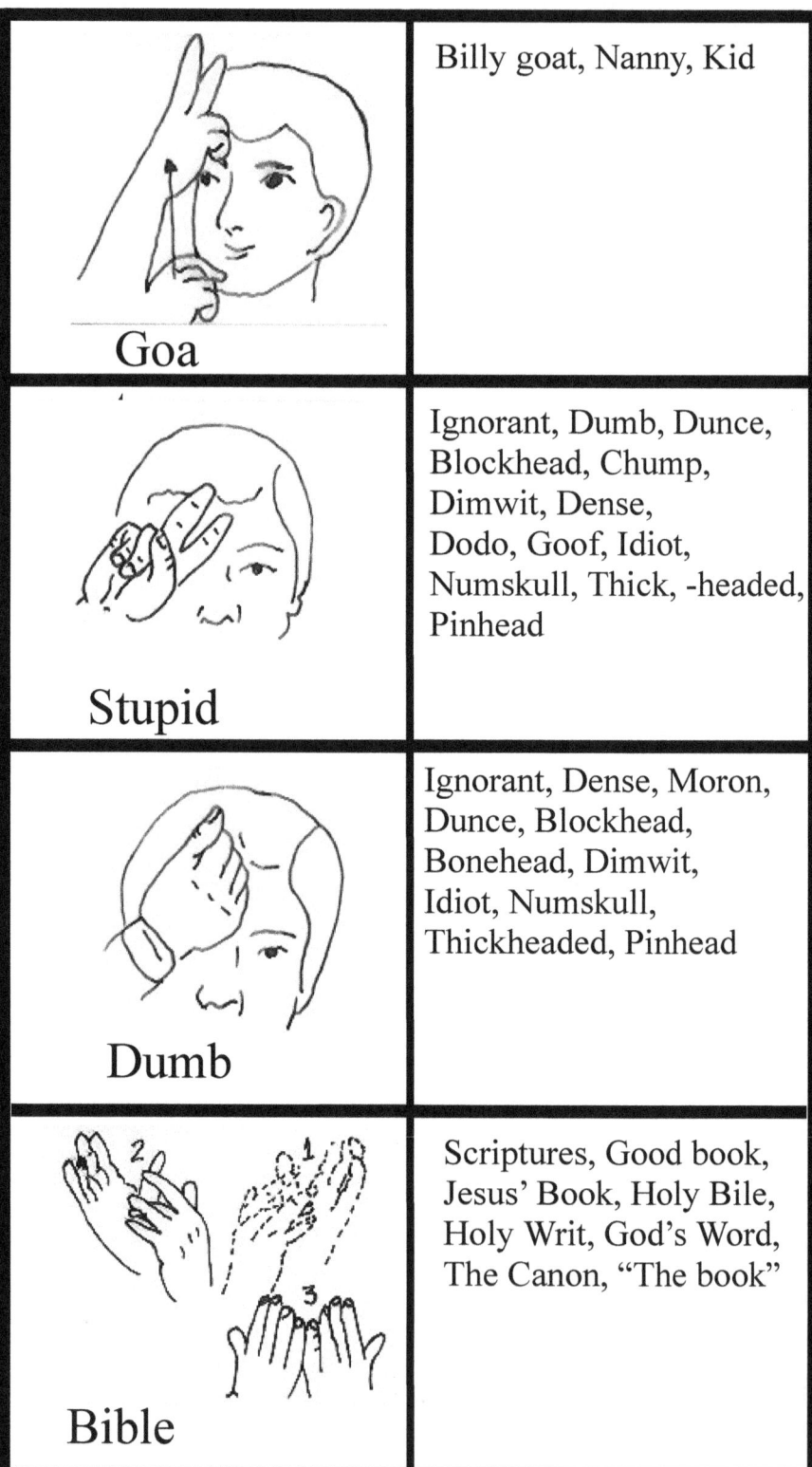

| | Billy goat, Nanny, Kid |

Goa

| | Ignorant, Dumb, Dunce, Blockhead, Chump, Dimwit, Dense, Dodo, Goof, Idiot, Numskull, Thick, -headed, Pinhead |

Stupid

| | Ignorant, Dense, Moron, Dunce, Blockhead, Bonehead, Dimwit, Idiot, Numskull, Thickheaded, Pinhead |

Dumb

| | Scriptures, Good book, Jesus' Book, Holy Bile, Holy Writ, God's Word, The Canon, "The book" |

Bible

Ma	Cross, Violent, Irritated, Cranky, Ticked off, Crabby, Provoked, Grumpy, Rabid, Ire, Irate, Aggravated, Furious, Enraged, Wrathful
Sa	Ejected, Sorrowful, Gloomy, Melancholy, Cast down, Unhappy, Remorse, Dismal, Mournful, Heavyhearted
Beautiful	Beauteous, Gorgeous, Ravishing, Exquisite, Awesome, Handsome, Divine
Prett	Beautiful, Lovely, Fair, Gorgeous, Attractive, Good looking, Ravishing, Comely, Handsome, Pulchritudinous, Stunning, Delightful

Ame	Worship, Adore, Sealed, Affirmed, So be it, I agree
Don't believe	Unbelief, Skeptical, Doubt
Se	Intimate, Relations, Marital relations, Intercourse, Love making
Camera	Take pictures, Photo

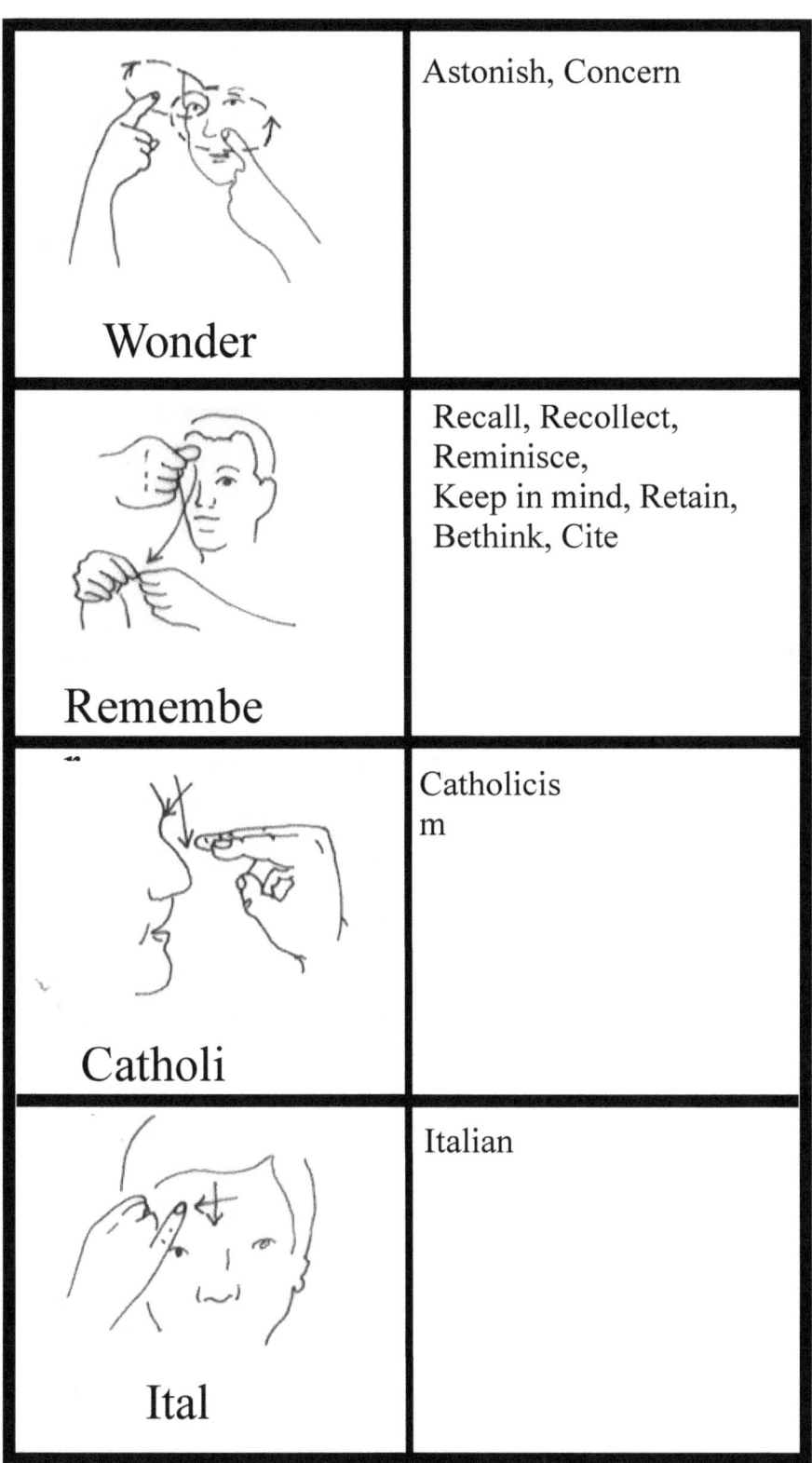

Wonder	Astonish, Concern
Remembe	Recall, Recollect, Reminisce, Keep in mind, Retain, Bethink, Cite
Catholi	Catholicis m
Ital	Italian

	Can't remember, Omit
Forget	
	Knowledge, Understand, Recognize, Perceive, Comprehend
Know	
	No cue, Not sure
Don't know	
	Due to, By reason of, In view of, 'cause, Inasmuch as, Whereas
Becaus	

	Wake up, Amazed, Awake, Aroused, Shocked, Stir, Prod, Rouse, Waken
Surprise	
d **Fac**	Look, Countenance, Appearance
e **Color**	Hue, Tint, Shade, Tone, Tinge, Pigment,Cast
Wh	What reason, How come, How so

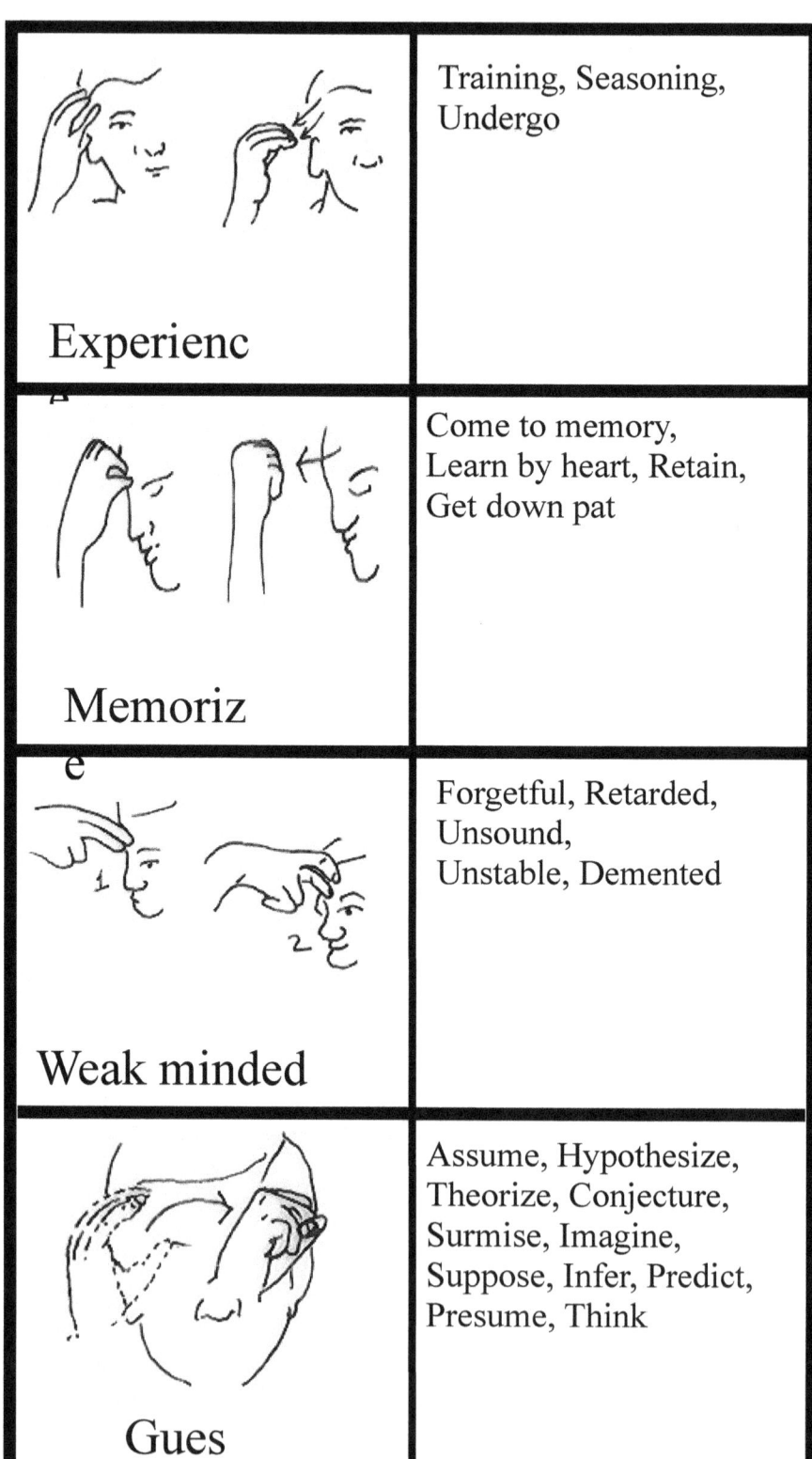

Experienc	Training, Seasoning, Undergo
Memoriz e	Come to memory, Learn by heart, Retain, Get down pat
Weak minded	Forgetful, Retarded, Unsound, Unstable, Demented
Gues	Assume, Hypothesize, Theorize, Conjecture, Surmise, Imagine, Suppose, Infer, Predict, Presume, Think

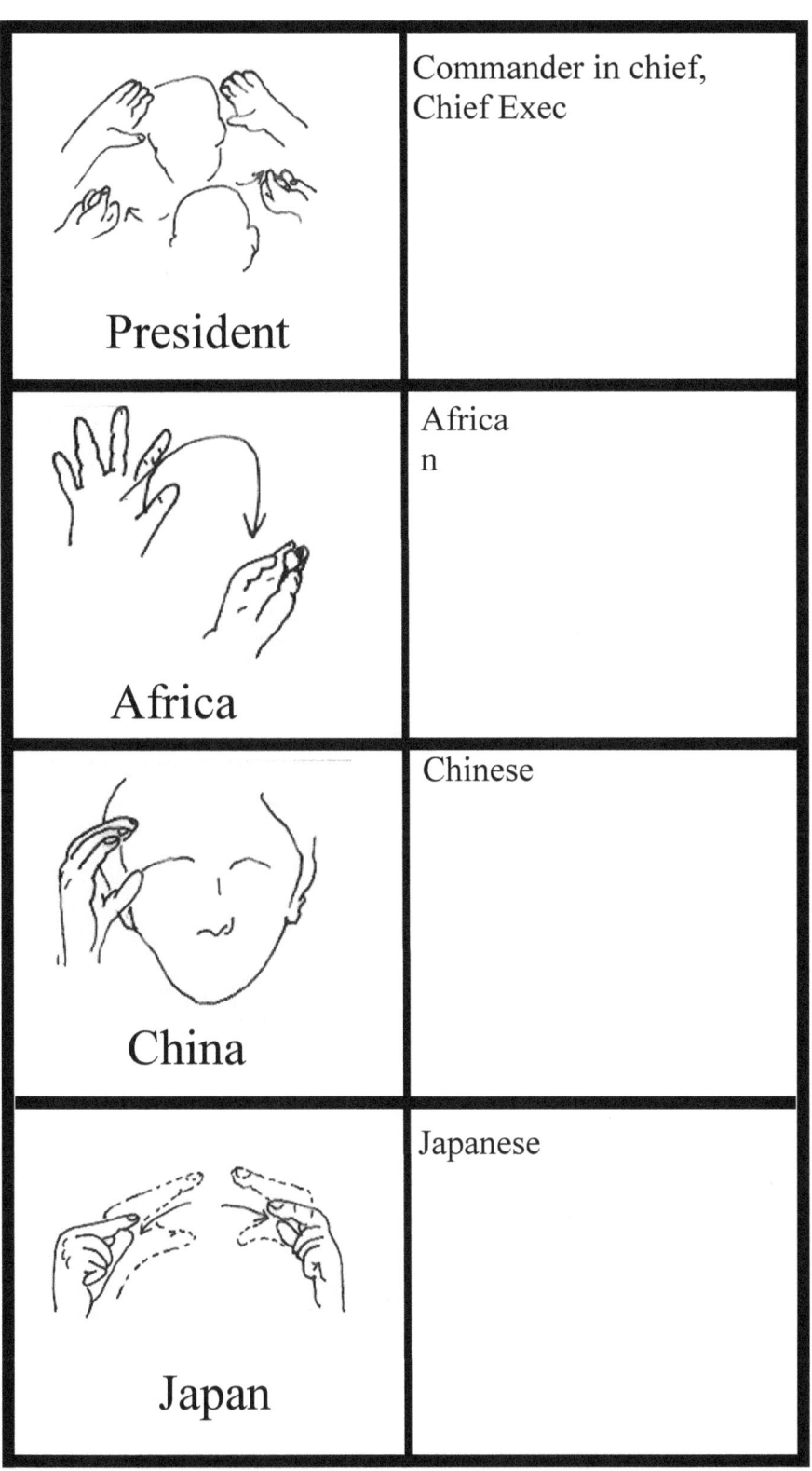

President	Commander in chief, Chief Exec
Africa	African
China	Chinese
Japan	Japanese

	Domain, Realm, Circle, Globe, Planed
World	
	Ridicule, Persecute, Irritate, Ruin, Taunt, Annoy, Spoil, Vex, Bedevil, Beleaguer, Harass, Needle, Pester, Harry, Aggravate, Tantalize
Tease	
	Done, Completed, Ended, Over, Already, Accomplished, Taken care of, Thorough, Concluded, Terminated, Wrapped up
Finished	
	Sociable, Neighborly, Cordial, Cheerful, Pleasant, Amiable, Harmonious, Gracious, Congenial, Amicable
Friendly	

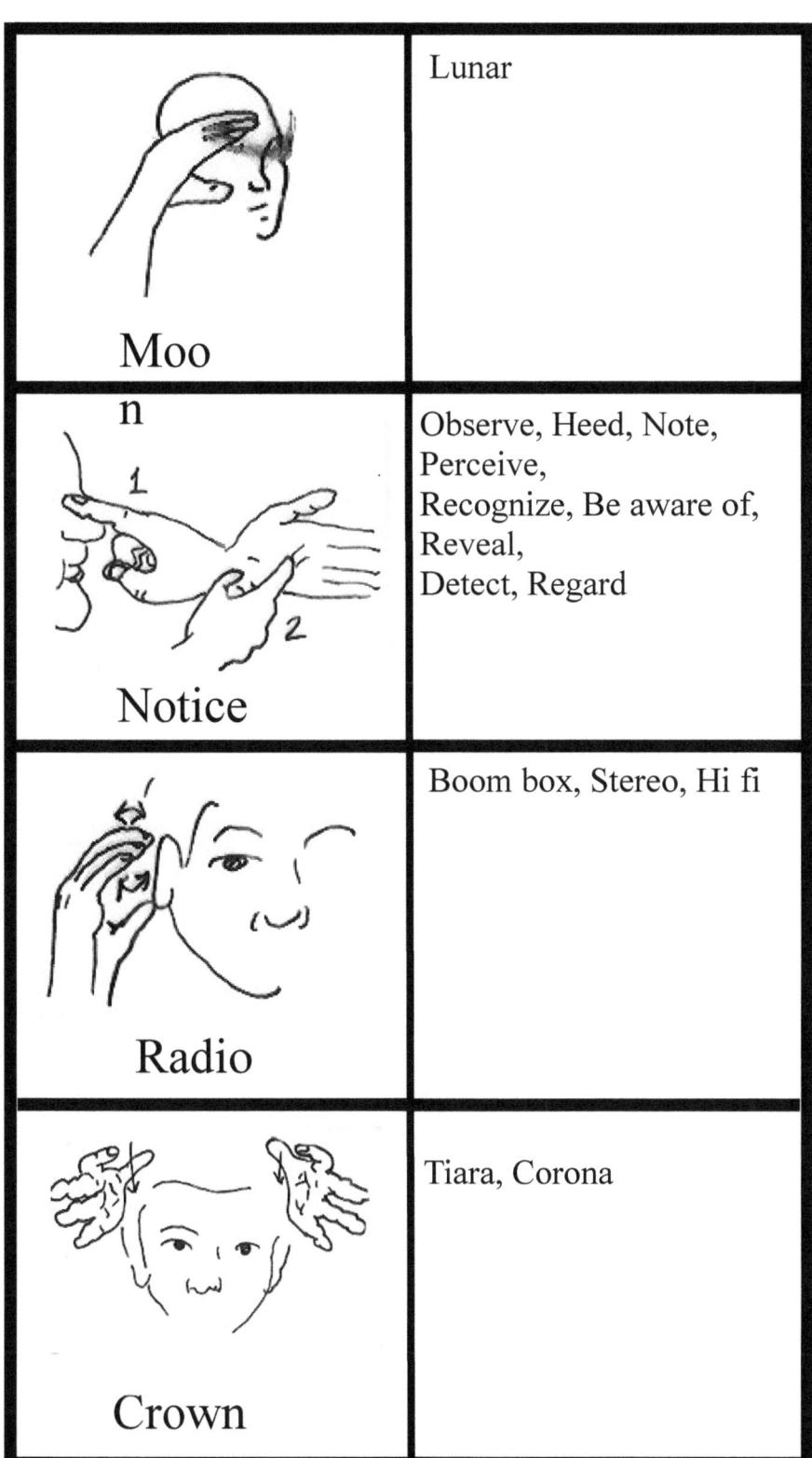

	Lunar
Moon	
Notice	Observe, Heed, Note, Perceive, Recognize, Be aware of, Reveal, Detect, Regard
Radio	Boom box, Stereo, Hi fi
Crown	Tiara, Corona

Plus	Also, Additional, Positive, Surplus, Coupled with
Minus	Negative, Less, Subtract, Deduct
Ren	Lease, Let, Charter, Hire
Take away	Minus, Withdrawal, To subtract, Abort

	Pupil, Apprentice, Scholar, Leaner, Disciple
Student	
	Hi, Greetings, Howdy, Salutations, Welcome, How
Hello	
	Trim, Buzz, Ears lowered
Haircu	
	Hair Salon, Beauty Salon
Beauty shop	

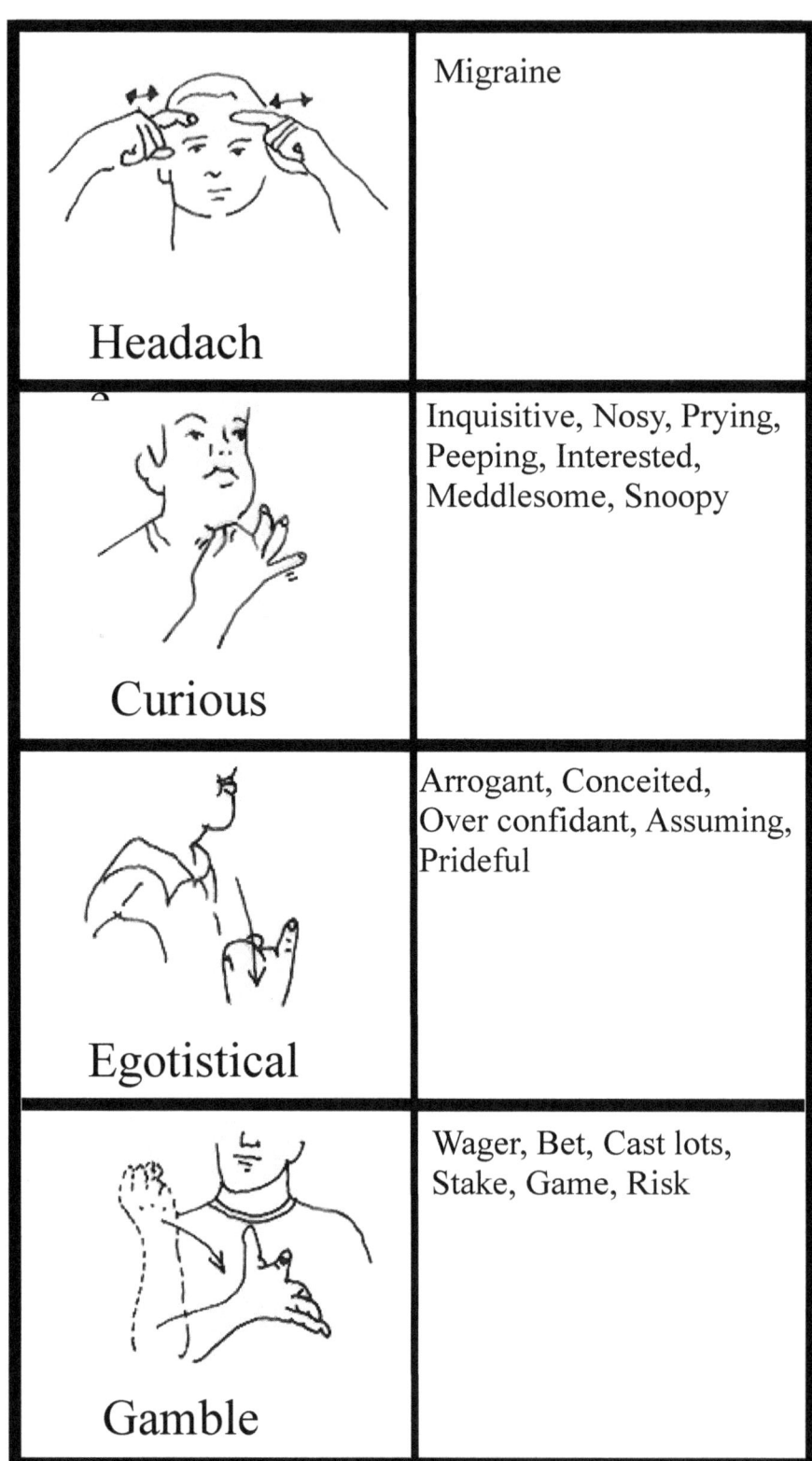

	Migraine
Headach	
Curious	Inquisitive, Nosy, Prying, Peeping, Interested, Meddlesome, Snoopy
Egotistical	Arrogant, Conceited, Over confidant, Assuming, Prideful
Gamble	Wager, Bet, Cast lots, Stake, Game, Risk

Profit	Benefit, Gain, Advantage, Prosper, Recover, Proceeds, Return
Drug	Dope, Narcotic, Pharmaceuticals, Opiates
Between	Among, Betwixt, Amid, Within, Tween, Twix
Seal	Stamp, Authorize, Sticker, Close, Approval, Permit, Allowance

	Turf, Green, Lawn, Yard
Grass	
Axe	Hatchet, Hack, Whack, Chop, Cut off
Feedbac	Contribute, Input, Constructive criticism
Pa	Payment, Compensate, Restitution, Wages, Refund, Salary, Award

	Tape player
Tape recorder	
converse	Talk, Speak to, Parley, Dialogue, Chat, Communicate, Discourse, Engage in conversation, Confabulate
Taxi	Cab
Roll	Revolve, Tumble, Turn, Turnover

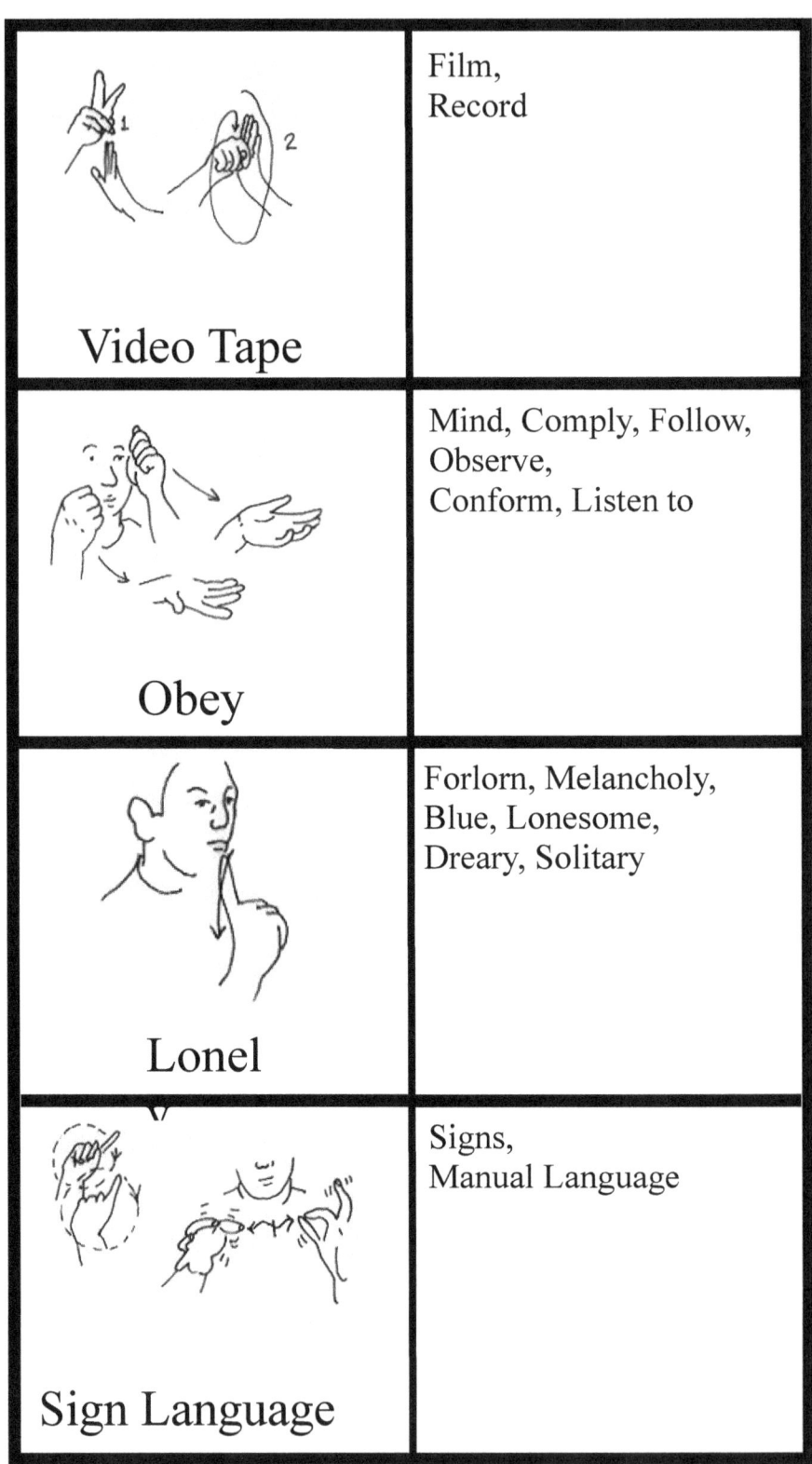

	Film, Record
Video Tape	
	Mind, Comply, Follow, Observe, Conform, Listen to
Obey	
	Forlorn, Melancholy, Blue, Lonesome, Dreary, Solitary
Lonely	
	Signs, Manual Language
Sign Language	

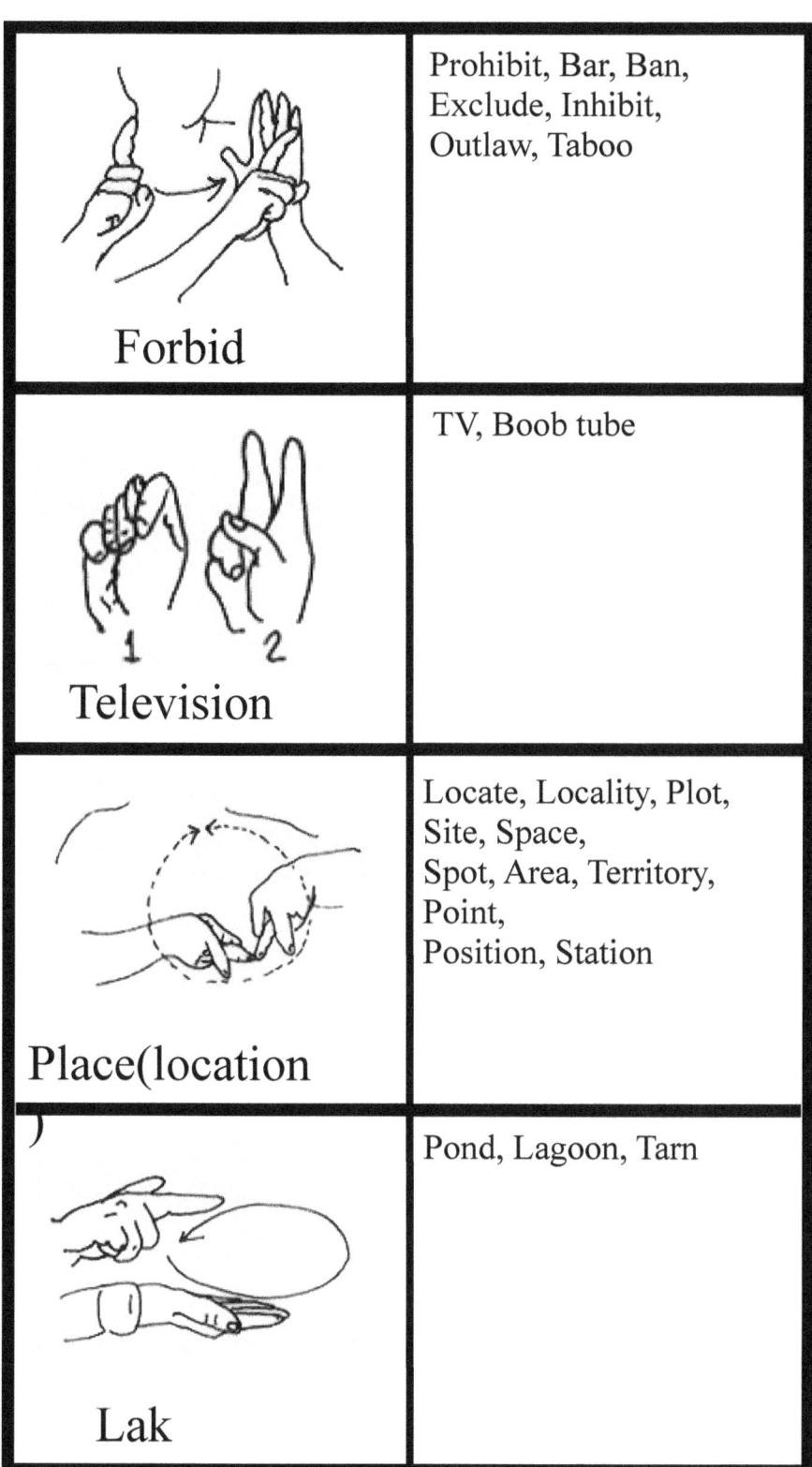

Forbid	Prohibit, Bar, Ban, Exclude, Inhibit, Outlaw, Taboo
Television	TV, Boob tube
Place(location)	Locate, Locality, Plot, Site, Space, Spot, Area, Territory, Point, Position, Station
Lak	Pond, Lagoon, Tarn

Multitud e	Crowd, Army, Gathering, Mob, Legion, Flock, Scores, Drove, Horde, Abundance
Bless	Favo r
Preach	Evangelize, Proclaim, Sermonize, Teach, Lecture
Grief	Sorrow, Anguish Bereavement, Distress, Depression, Vexation, Woe,Torment, Heartache, Crushed, Affliction, Rud

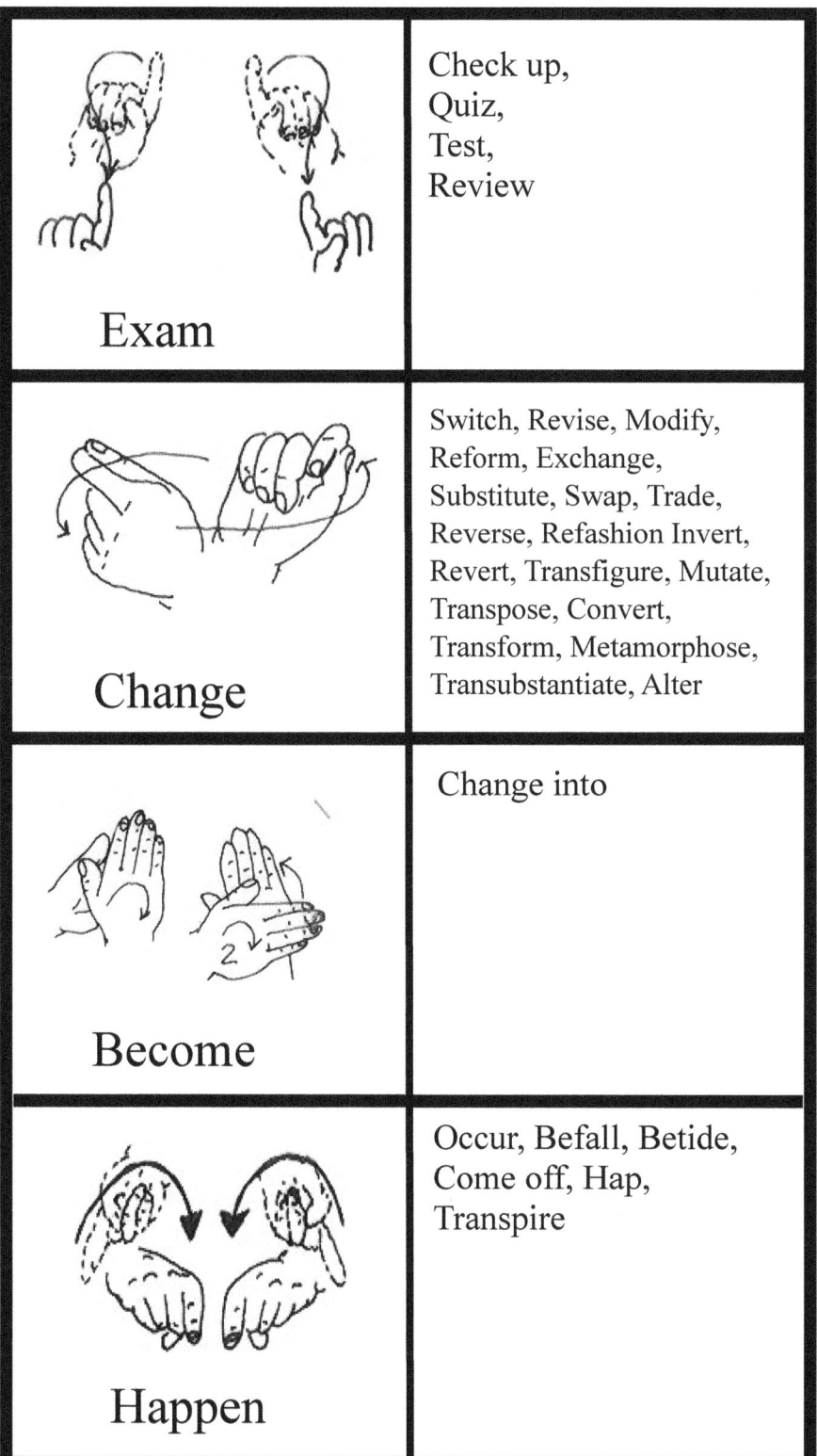

Exam	Check up, Quiz, Test, Review
Change	Switch, Revise, Modify, Reform, Exchange, Substitute, Swap, Trade, Reverse, Refashion Invert, Revert, Transfigure, Mutate, Transpose, Convert, Transform, Metamorphose, Transubstantiate, Alter
Become	Change into
Happen	Occur, Befall, Betide, Come off, Hap, Transpire

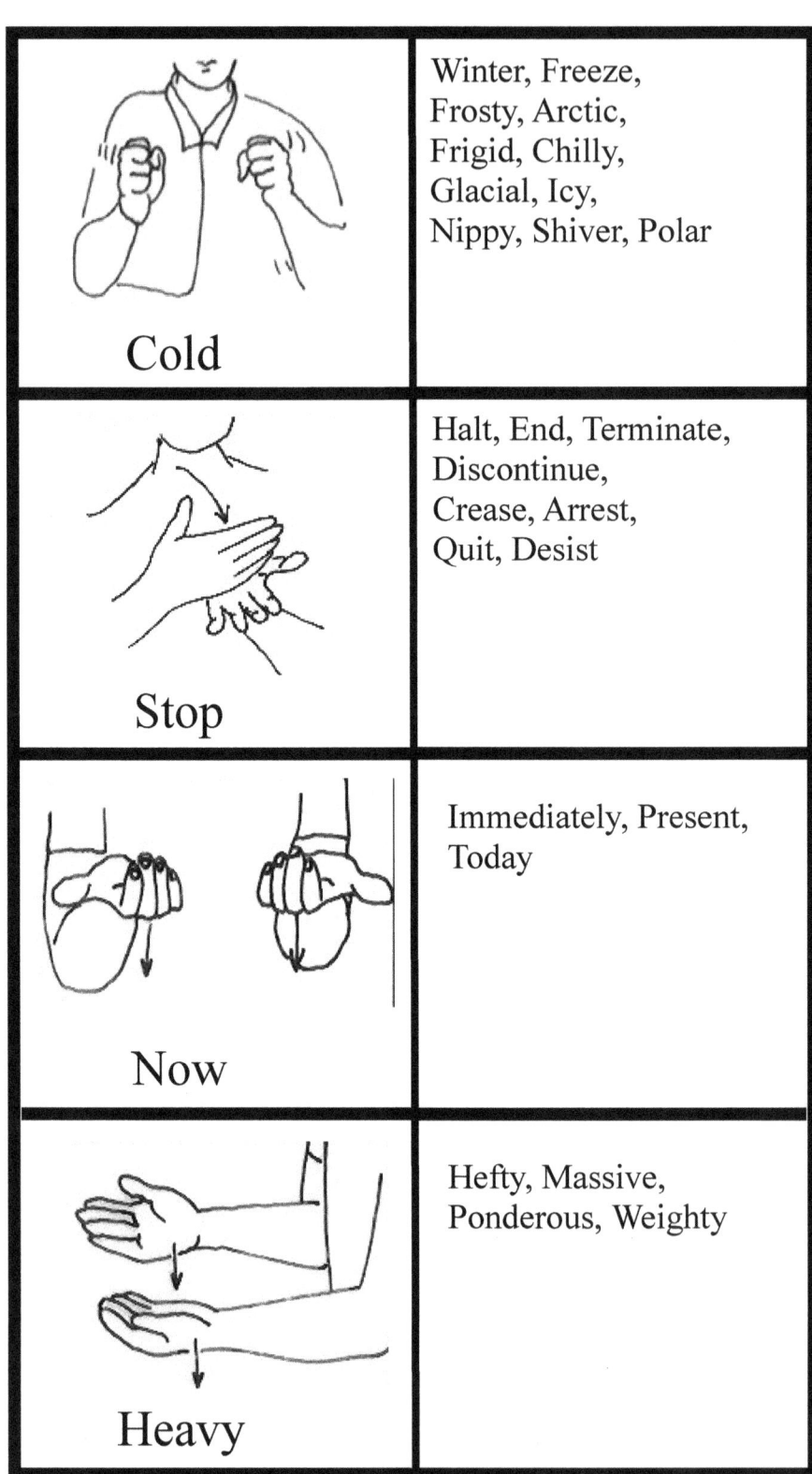

Cold	Winter, Freeze, Frosty, Arctic, Frigid, Chilly, Glacial, Icy, Nippy, Shiver, Polar
Stop	Halt, End, Terminate, Discontinue, Crease, Arrest, Quit, Desist
Now	Immediately, Present, Today
Heavy	Hefty, Massive, Ponderous, Weighty

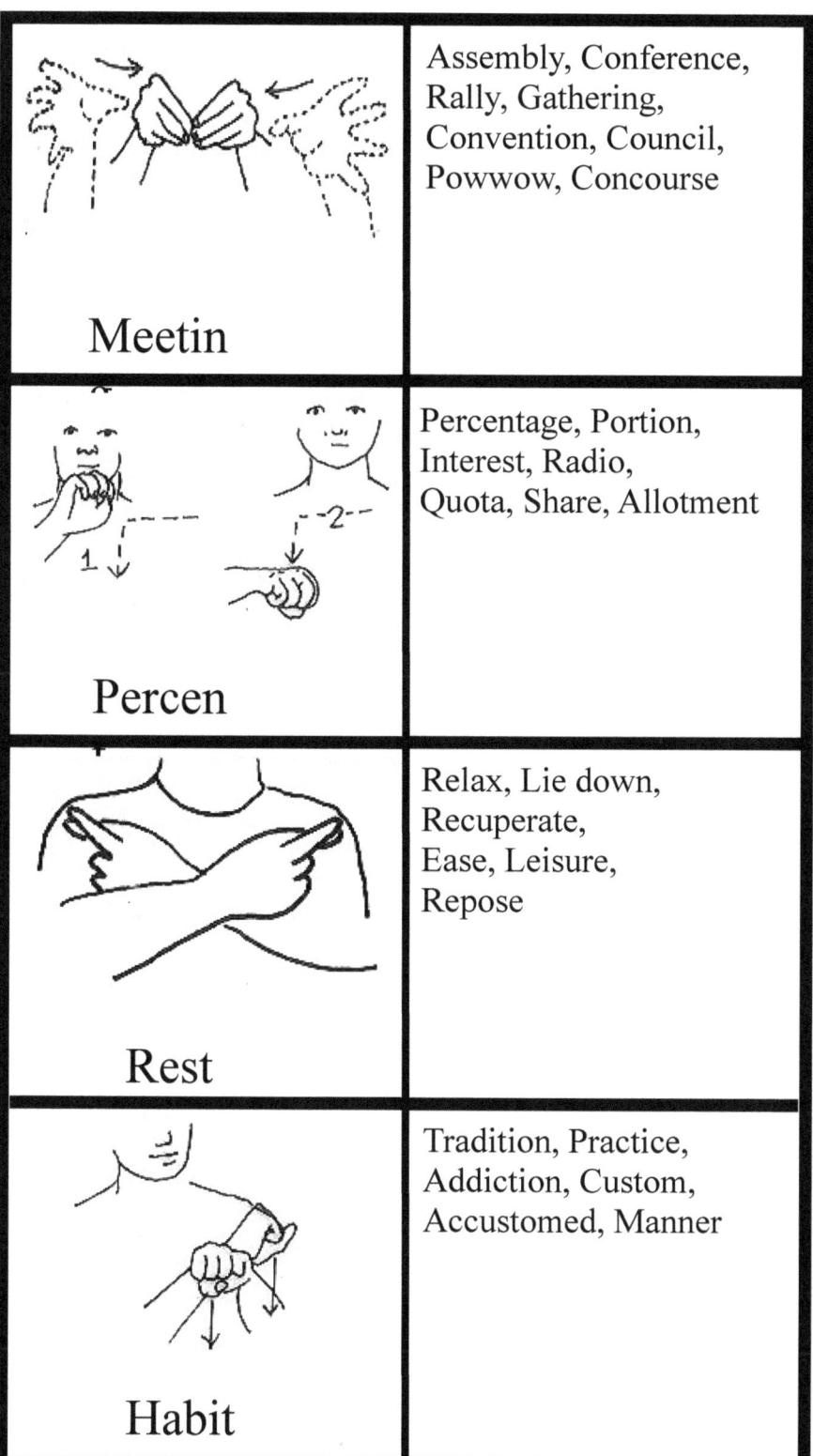

	Assembly, Conference, Rally, Gathering, Convention, Council, Powwow, Concourse
Meetin	
	Percentage, Portion, Interest, Radio, Quota, Share, Allotment
Percen	
	Relax, Lie down, Recuperate, Ease, Leisure, Repose
Rest	
	Tradition, Practice, Addiction, Custom, Accustomed, Manner
Habit	

www.ingramcontent.com/pod-product-compliance
Lightning Source LLC
Chambersburg PA
CBHW051145120626
46547CB00012B/952